Finding Herself There

Melissa L. Ross

abbott press

This book is a work of non-fiction. Unless otherwise noted, the author
and the publisher make no explicit guarantees as to the accuracy of
the information contained in this book and in some cases, names of
people and places have been altered to protect their privacy.

: Scripture quotations marked NIV are taken from the Holy Bible, New
International Version. NIV. Copyright 1973, 1978, 1984 by International
Bible Society. Used by permission of Zondervan. All rights reserved.

Abbott Press books may be ordered through booksellers or by contacting:

Abbott Press
1663 Liberty Drive
Bloomington, IN 47403
www.abbottpress.com
Phone: 1 (866) 697-5310

Because of the dynamic nature of the Internet, any web addresses or
links contained in this book may have changed since publication and
may no longer be valid. The views expressed in this work are solely those
of the author and do not necessarily reflect the views of the publisher,
and the publisher hereby disclaims any responsibility for them.

Any people depicted in stock imagery provided by Thinkstock are models,
and such images are being used for illustrative purposes only.
Certain stock imagery © Thinkstock.

ISBN: 978-1-4582-2117-9 (sc)
ISBN: 978-1-4582-2116-2 (e)

Library of Congress Control Number: 2017910515

Print information available on the last page.

Abbott Press rev. date: 07/13/2017

THE MEANING OF THE SPIRAL

The spiral is one of the oldest symbols in human spirituality. Although it can have various meanings, many believe that it represents movement through life experiences as a symbol of expansion, personal growth and development. As we make our journey to the center, we discover spiritual balance. This helps us recognize that we are all deeply connected to the external forces of nature, the universe, and each other. It starts as an outward perception of external awareness and leads inward as an unbroken path that is constantly in motion. The more we look inward, the better we can understand our outer world. As we discover, know and understand ourselves, we discover, know and understand others because of this interconnectedness.

We may feel like we are going around in circles in life, often ending up where we started, but we are never the same as when we began because each experience we have, and each person we meet, changes us in some way. For me, the spiral illustrates that our journeys in life are not linear, but circular, as a winding road to truly knowing ourselves as well as the world around us. On our journeys to finding ourselves, we also find each other.

ACKNOWLEDGEMENTS

Special thanks to my mother, Sandie Ross. I am forever grateful for the way you have always encouraged me, believed in me, loved me unconditionally, and never gave up on me. I love you, Mom, and I could not have found myself without you.

Special thanks to my amazing partner, Katie Roche, for unconditionally loving me, for diligently editing this book, and for being someone I can truly call home. You are my forever soulmate and I am so glad I found you along my journey.

It would be remiss of me to not also thank all the people who have helped me along my journey. Each person we meet truly is our teacher. Some of the people I have met have helped show me who I want to be and some people I have met have shown me who I do *not* want to be, but I am thankful to them all because each has helped shape me in some way to be the person I am today.

Last, but certainly not least, thanks to everyone who has read my first memoir, *Surviving Crazy: A Roadmap To The Scars,* and thanks to those who were interested enough to give this second book a chance as well. Sharing our painful struggles with each other along our journeys not only helps lighten the burden, but can also help us to not feel so alone. Sharing our triumphs with each other along our journey not only encourages others to keep trudging, but can help to be a light along other's paths as well. I believe the purpose of life is not a solitary journey of finding and eventually loving yourself, but to also help others along their way to do the same. To quote Ram Dass, "We are all just walking each other home."[1] I realize that the definition of home varies with each person's belief. However, I feel that it's not as important where "home" is to any one of us, even if you believe that we simply return to dust when we die, because life is more about the journey rather than the destination. I truly hope sharing my journey and what I've learned along the way helps people. Even if it helps just one person, it will have been worth it.

Remember, you are not given the right to be happy. You are only given the right to "pursue happiness." Once we learn to stop madly trying to "pursue it" and discover how to be happy where we are right now, along our paths, we finally realize it was always about the journey, rather than the destination, anyway.

WHEN A PERSON CAN LISTEN TO ANOTHER'S "STORY" WITHOUT BEING TRIGGERED TO DEFEND OR VOICE THEIR OWN, IT IS THEN THAT THEY ARE ON THE ROAD TO ENLIGHTENMENT. FOR IT IS THEIR STORY AND THEIR TRUTH, WHICH DOESN'T HAVE TO BE YOURS.

FOREWORD

"The desire to help others overcome life's deepest, darkest, sometimes cruelest obstacles really shines through in Melissa's writing. She writes with pure honesty and intelligence using her own life's circumstances to illustrate to people that they are not alone when struggling with the terrible feelings that depression can create. It has been a long, hard road for her, yet she has always held onto her ability to fight. What you read is what she is about, simple as that. She manages to interject humor when she can, although, as her mother, I know she continues to struggle to this day. I have always been extremely proud of her for standing up not only for what she believes, but for standing beside others who cannot stand, and helping them to have the strength to carry on. My love for her is endless."

With much love and admiration, Mom

FINDING HERSELF THERE

Warning: This book is full of my opinions, thoughts, feelings, and beliefs. Sometimes topics are random and ideas may seem scattered. This is done on purpose because you aren't just reading a book, you are entering my mind. Please remember that. Also, I encourage others to have open minds, think for themselves, and challenge their way of thinking. However, it's deeply important to me for people to know that I do not share my opinions and beliefs in judgment of others. Nor do I condemn or expect to change their beliefs. While I might suggest alternative ways of thinking, by sharing what I have learned through my experiences, the main reason I share my story is with the hope that it might help others to not feel so alone. There's healing power in "Hey, me, too!" and that sincerely is the purpose of this book. *Finding Herself There* roughly picks up where my first memoir, *Surviving Crazy: A Roadmap to the Scars* (2013), left off, but this book is more of a narrated journey of self-discovery and enlightenment rather than memoir continuation.

> *"None of us can speak the Truth; we can*
> *only speak our own truths."*
> -Melissa Ross

People are always trying to "*find themselves*." That's why self-help books continue to be so popular. I have "found myself" many times throughout my life. I have found myself waking up in a mental institution, not having any idea how I got there, only to find out later that I drove the two-hour drive there myself in a total blackout. I have found myself waking up from a drunken stupor, in a motel sleeping room, next to a man I hardly even knew and thought, "What the fuck am I doing here?" I have found myself being arrested by the police. I have found myself feeling so excited, so high, so manic that I started developing a detailed plan to jump off a bridge into the river, knowing that I would survive because God loved me and if I didn't survive, that would mean that He obviously did not love me. I have also found myself feeling so low, so dark, so depressed, so hopeless that I developed another, yet different, detailed plan, which was to end my life, because I couldn't take the emotional pain and sadness one more minute.

This, of course, is a play on words. I never really "found myself" in any of those places in my past, meaning I never discovered who I truly was during any of those times. I think this is because I wasn't being or searching for my authentic self. Maybe you've heard the theoretical reasoning as to why your rearview mirror in your psychological car is way smaller than your windshield. The saying goes, "Don't look back. You're not going that way."[2] I must say that I do not believe in never looking back. Some people might think that works for them, but I have found that it does not work for me. I have found that it's important to look back on my life because it can explain so much. It can give me the answers that I need, answers that looking forward would not give me.

I'm not talking about blaming people or circumstances for being the way I am today. There's a difference between blaming and discovering the possible reasons and causes as to why you are the way you are. If I can see where I might have gone a little wrong, then maybe that can help me from repeating the same wrongs. If I can make things make sense in my head, as to maybe how I got "here," I can work with those explanations, creating a baseline for myself from which to move forward and grow. Figuring out the possible "whys" of your life can give you encouragement to be different in your future. It's not about holding onto resentments, which I admit, to an extent I still do. Yes, I realize that I'm "drinking the poison meant for my enemies," but I am still working on that.

On the surface, I have "found myself" a lot during the 46 years that I've been on this earth so far. And really, isn't that what it's all about? Finding yourself? That's, at least, what I believed, because that's what I had been told. That's what I had read in all the self-help books, too. The thing about finding yourself, though, is first you must *know* yourself. You must know who you are, know who you are looking for and who you want to *find* when you start on any quest to "find yourself."

Before you go looking behind the couch cushions or take a trip into the wild, it's important to know WHO you are looking for. I mean, it only makes sense, right? You can't go looking for someone you don't know, right? How will you know when you find her? Will she be wearing a name badge? Will she call out to you, amid the crowd, waving her hand wildly, shouting, "I'm over here!" Doubtfully.

So, it feels like putting the cart before the horse, but since you must know who you are looking for to find yourself, you must first know yourself. And I don't think it stops at knowing who you are, to find yourself. You then have to accept who you are. Because if you find yourself, waving madly in that sea of people, and you don't accept that that is in fact you, wouldn't you feel like averting your eyes from your shouting self and act like you don't know her, turning briskly to walk the other way? Notice I didn't say LIKE yourself, which is different from accepting yourself. You don't have to like a person to accept who they are. Maybe she's an asshole. You don't like her, but you accept that. You accept her.

Knowing and accepting who you are is often a very hard thing to accomplish. You might be thinking as I did at first, "I have no idea who I am!" Before you get discouraged and throw this book on the ground, hold on, because there is good news. The best part about not knowing who you are is that you then get to decide who you want to be. *Carte blanche*, so to speak…a blank slate. It can be hard to start where you are at. Accepting your current life situation, accepting who you are, at the start, is really the first step in creating a new you who you can believe in again, or even start to believe in for the very first time. Making peace with what your life looks like at the beginning moment of your journey can help you to see more clearly as to what led to the life situation that you are in right now. Resistance and fighting with your situation will only impede your progress and will not do you any good. Acceptance first gives us the energy we need for the journey.

"First accept sadness. Realize that without losing, winning isn't so great." - Alyssa Milano[3]

After acceptance and acknowledgement, we can wipe the slate clean to begin again on defining who we really want to be. In order to know who, you really want to be, you must ask yourself what are your likes and dislikes. What triggers you? These are the areas you want to work on changing. What makes you so passionate that you would stand up and fight? These are your strengths because they are your core beliefs about yourself and life in general. Just remember that you are the one in control. You are the one and only one who gets to decide who you will be and who you want to be. And let me say that it doesn't matter if other people think they know who you are. Some will even gladly and readily tell you who you are, but you don't have to believe them. They might know who they think you are, know who they want you to be, or most likely, how they perceive you to be, but they do not entirely know the whole, real you.

Never let anyone else define who you are by accepting other people telling you who you are, or by you comparing yourself to them. Again, you and only you get to decide that. That's your power. So, the next question is, who do you want to be? Who do you think you are or might be? Is how you see yourself an accurate account of who you truly are? I came to a point in my life, so tired of trying to find myself, that the idea finally occurred to me that maybe I should stop looking? Maybe I didn't truly *want* to find myself? Maybe I was afraid of who I would find, once I found me. That's when it hit me, how will I even know me when I find me? WHO AM I? Who do I want to be? Who do I want to find? These were unanswered questions up until this point in my life. Getting to know yourself must include the good, the bad, and the ugly if it is to be a complete and honest vision of who you are. And now I drop the bomb on you. This mission, this venture to find yourself, isn't a one-time journey. The reason it's not a one-time search is because we are constantly changing who we are. I am not only talking about huge changes, which sometimes happen, too, but not always. I'm also talking about the slight, little changes that you intend or don't intend on happening.

In April of 2013, I wrote my first book. On the surface, a person might think that my memoir, *Surviving Crazy: A Roadmap to the Scars*, was a book about finding myself. However, most of the book was actually about *running away* from myself. I'm not talking about a light jog, either. I'm talking about running like a Spaniard running from angry bulls. It was fleeing, quite honestly. I was fleeing the scenes of my life that were too hard to watch, running away so fast and so hard that I was completely exhausted and breathless. Right up until the end of the book, that is. I tried so very hard to run away from myself, from who I was, from who I wasn't, I just wanted to get the hell away from me. I tried to escape myself and the pain of being me by drinking, taking drugs, being sexually involved with people who clearly were not good for me, even self-mutilation. I would do just about anything to numb the thoughts and feelings that I had, especially about myself, because I didn't see any good in me. I only saw bad. I only saw suffering and pain. I couldn't just feel my feelings, or think my thoughts, and then let them go, like many people can. I would get stuck in my thoughts and emotions. I wouldn't just get stuck. It was more like I would get enveloped, and swallowed whole by them. I hated myself and just wanted to get the fuck away from myself.

So, I ran. I ran figuratively and I ran literally. Then I heard the saying, "Wherever you go, there you are."[4] Once I realized that no matter what I did, I couldn't escape myself,

I stopped. Once I realized no one could help me escape myself, no one could change what I hated so badly about myself, no one could save me, I stopped. I knew my running was pointless because it was a circular race track that would always just lead me back to the beginning, after running so hard and for so long. I knew then I had to "own my shit, face my shit, and get my shit together" if I was ever going to be happy with whom I found at the end of my race. And I am certainly not suggesting that this was an easy task. I had to take a cold, hard look at my beginning, where I started, and how I might have gotten myself there. I had to put appropriate blame where it belonged, too. I was blaming myself for things that were not my fault, things that were completely out of my control. And I was not taking accountability of the things for which I was responsible, my bad choices in my life.

I knew I couldn't do this alone, though. I knew I had to get help, or start taking the help that was offered to me much more seriously. I didn't expect people to fix me after that. I accepted the fact that I needed the right guidance from the right people, but I knew I was the one who had to do the work to get there. I started owning some things about myself. I faced that ugly baseline start and decided who I wanted to be. I made up my mind who I wanted to find, and slowly, but with determination, I began the true journey.

So, you could say the last several pages of my first book were about finding myself. I feel that it definitely illustrated how a person changes, but what is an even better example of that was what happened to me a year after I wrote my memoir. I found myself again. I found myself getting 20 shock treatments to my head in a psychiatric hospital. I was so glad that I titled that first memoir *"Surviving Crazy"* instead of *"Survived Crazy,"* because as mentally healthy as I was at the end of that book, I knew my journeys on finding myself weren't over. That's also part of the nature of the beast that's called bipolar disorder.

I didn't know this on my first journey out, and I'm not trying to be a pessimist, but I have come to realize and accept that my bipolar disorder is not something that I can survive with a "d" on the end. Spoiler alert to my fellow sufferers who don't know this but, there is no cure. However, on the brighter side, a person who suffers with bipolar disorder can have their disease go into remission. In fact, it can go into remission for years. It's unlikely that it will go into remission, though, if it's not addressed by medication and therapy. But you can survive it daily, doing those things that are within your power to do, such as the choosing to get help through therapy and/or medication.

I would love to be writing this second book about my entire, detailed experience during the time I was getting electroconvulsive therapy, because it might be helpful to others to share with them what it was like, but I can't. I can't because ECT destroys part of your memory. This still really upsets me because as I stated before, I find that looking back in retrospect is a helpful thing to know where you might look for yourself next. I do not remember things like the car ride down to the hospital, what my hospital room looked like, who my roommate was, what I did all day, every day, while I was there for two weeks, where I went to the bathroom and showered, what I ate, who visited me, how I survived the two weeks without cigarettes, and other details like that. For some of my memories, I count on my mother and partner to tell me what it was like for me, from their memories of the whole thing. I will share with you those things as well as what I do remember, and maybe it will be of at least some help to others.

Around the beginning of 2014, my mood took a huge turn for the worse. I discussed this with this my psychiatrist and she determined that the medications that I was taking seemed to have stopped working. She tried various other medications over the next several months, but none of them made any difference and did not work. As I descended into yet another bottomless hole of depression, I found myself making plans again. These were not good plans. I mean, they felt like very good plans to me at the time. They actually felt like the only plans that I had to make. The plan to finally end my torment became the only thing I could focus on. I used to say that the worst thing about having depression and feeling depressed isn't feeling suicidal and wanting to kill yourself. The worst part of having depression and feeling depressed is feeling suicidal and knowing that suicide, ending your suffering, cannot be an option because of the people you love and who love you. But I sunk deeper than that belief by September of 2014.

For the record, I do not believe that suicide is a selfish act. Those left behind might think that, but it's truly about the incessant need to end one's pain and suffering. What those left behind sometimes don't understand is that a person who ends their life just couldn't do it anymore. I feel safe in saying that those who have killed themselves all tried, tried their very hardest in fact, to hang on because of not wanting to hurt those who loved them. It's not a spontaneous act. A lot of thought and feeling went into my plan to finally find relief. Towards the end of that year, 2014, my plans were so solidified that they scared me. I knew that I had to put myself in a place that I could not execute my plan, solely because of how much I loved my family and friends and didn't want to hurt them. So, I asked my mother and partner to take me to the hospital. My psychiatrist and therapist insisted on it, as well. I knew I needed more help to fight myself than I could do on the outside. I remember feeling that incessant, strong urge to run again. I didn't know to where I would run, but I wanted to run far away from being put back into a psychiatric hospital. I wanted to flee as fast as I could from the terrifying idea of getting my brain shocked. I couldn't figure out how I got in this position again, but instead of running, I remembered, "wherever you go, there you are." Somehow, I had lost myself in the madness of depression and I knew I had to find myself again.

They tell me that all I did was cry, completely curled up in the back seat of the car during the hour trip to the safe place of the psychiatric hospital. They also tell me that maybe it's good that I don't remember most of it. My mother and partner suggest that maybe it's just too painful for me to revisit and think about. I think my disrupted memory is more about having electrical current sent through my brain than a self-protection mechanism in my head, but no one really knows for sure. All I do know is that I was depressed enough, desperate enough, to agree to the terrifying idea of electroconvulsive therapy, so it must have been bad.

To those readers whom I may have disappointed by not being able to make this book a direct continuation of my first memoir, I will try to squint into the rearview mirror a bit more. I don't remember what, if anything, triggered the depressive episode I found myself in at the beginning of 2014, but I know it was a gradual descent. For some reason, only parts of my brain know, I started getting those thoughts again. I thought I was focused on forward, after writing my memoir. It felt so good to relieve myself of those secrets that were keeping me sick. The thing about revealing your darkest secrets, your shame, your guilt, your mistakes and transgressions, is that no one can use them against you if you admit them and take accountability for your part in them. I was in therapy, working hard on my issues. I was taking my medications as prescribed, yet something was happening again in my brain. Out of nowhere, those devious, devouring thoughts started coming in and I started to get tired. It's a tired feeling that only those who have experienced depression can truly understand. You just get tired and then more tired and the struggle starts over. No amount of sleep helped my exhausted soul. Effort became a hassle and those incessant thoughts made that drained feeling wear me down even more.

Those dark thoughts continued. I did fight them at first, and continued to fight them for a long time, but there comes a time where you just get too exhausted to combat them any longer. They were solidifying in my head, becoming more real as the days went on. I struggled and fought the good fight with them, I really did, but I got to a point where I just had no fight left in me. I was broken down and so tired physically, mentally, emotionally, spiritually, every way you could be tired, I felt exhausted at it. They tell me that I stopped talking to people. I stopped even trying to connect, stopped even trying to get the crazy shit out of me. It was consuming me to where the only logical thing for me to do, in my mind, was to put an end to it.

My thoughts went from irrational to delusional. I truly never ever want to hurt my loved ones by ending my life. I never want to do that to them because I sincerely do love them so very much. So, there I found myself, in the emergency waiting room of the psychiatric hospital, waiting for them to find a bed for me. We waited there for over 6 hours, with me sobbing, distraught, curled up in the fetal position between my mother and my partner, till they told me they found a bed for me. It was on the eating disorder unit of the hospital, but I didn't care. I didn't have an eating disorder, but as long as I was admitted to the psychiatric hospital, I knew they could at least start the ECT treatments there. Having to be placed on the eating disorder unit proved to be quite ironic later, but I don't want to get ahead of my story.

An online social media friend recently wrote me a message, revealing that she was really struggling with her depression. Knowing that I had gone through electroconvulsive therapy, she wanted to know if I recommended ECT. This is what I told her: To be completely honest, the ECT treatments were my last resort, because I was seriously going to kill myself. Somehow, I mustered the strength to know I had to put myself in the hospital and try the treatments because, as I have said, I did not want to devastate my Mom, my partner Katie, and the other people who loved me by subjecting them to my suicide. I was truthfully scared shitless, though. In my past and right up to the point that I allowed myself to be committed to the psychiatric hospital, I swore I would never get shock treatments.

I researched ECT before I was even taken to the hospital and read all kind of horrifying things that could happen while receiving the treatments, such as that you had to wear a diaper when you got the treatments because your bowels evacuate themselves each time your brain is subjected to the electrical current shocks. This, by the way, is not true, or at least was not my experience. I did not have to wear a diaper and the ECT did not cause my bowels to release themselves, nor did my bladder. My whole body also did not convulse, my toes didn't curl, and they did not have to put anything in my mouth to prevent me from biting off my tongue. All those things did used to happen years ago, when ECT was first discovered. However, it's not like you will be wheeled out afterwards, looking like Jack Nicholson's character in the movie, *One Flew Over the Cuckoo's Nest*, as I had previously thought before I experienced ECT for myself. It's not a lobotomy. They don't remove part of your brain, leaving you with that blank, emotionless stare.

ECT involves wires hooked up to your head, sending electrical current through your brain. Thankfully, doctors have made many advancements since ECT first was attempted to help a mentally ill person. There was no convulsing because they gave me a muscle relaxer and sedations, through IV, so I could avoid that horrible part. It's so weird that I don't remember much from being in the hospital for those two weeks. I know that I slept a lot because they kept me on a high dose of Ativan to keep me calm, which made me feel a bit like a zombie. I was so terrified of agreeing to get the ECT treatments that my psychiatrist and therapist wanted me to get. This was probably the scariest thing I ever went through in my 44 years of existence.

I explained to my friend that I had to be in the hospital for about two weeks to get the first several ECT treatments, but then I could get the remaining treatments on an outpatient basis. However, someone had to drive me there, since I wasn't allowed to drive the entire time I was receiving the treatments. Before each treatment, they would take me into a room to be evaluated by the nurse. She would ask me questions like, What's my name? Where was I? What year is it? And she would always give me a grouping of words, such as truck, flower, red, three, and dog. Then, she would tell me to try to remember those five words for later in the conversation, asking me to then recall them. There were three sets of these groups of words, so she did mix it up a bit each time. It was clear that my memory was greatly damaged by the shock treatments, but I was told that some of my memory could come back and that in time, my short-term memory would get better.

After being in the hospital for those first two weeks, receiving treatments, I was thrilled the day they told me that they were releasing me from the hospital to continue the treatments on an outpatient basis. For the next three months, I received more shock treatments. All I can really remember is getting into a hospital gown, each time, lying down on a gurney in a room with about five other people each lying on their own gurney, all lined up to wait their turn to go into the smaller ECT room where several doctors and nurses were waiting to administer the treatments. I truly felt like a lamb in line to be slaughtered. When it was my turn I would be rolled into the little room on the gurney with the doctors and nurses surrounding me as they started to hook me up to the machine. I had several electrodes placed around my head and they monitored my heart as well. The medicine would be injected into my IV and I usually only made it to number 97 in my countdown from 100 before I was under anesthesia and completely out of it. The next thing I knew,

I would wake up in the recovery room, put my clothes back on, and was told that I could go home. I remember even having to get ECT on my birthday. I was so very thankful and grateful to have my partner help me through all of this. Katie was so loving, so supportive and she drove me to my outpatient ECT appointments. I could not have survived this experience without the unconditional love and support of her and my mother. My mom was so encouraging, loving, and supportive, too, always trying to keep my spirits up. Their undying faith in me gave me the courage and strength to not give up during this entire process.

After each treatment, you are in recovery for about an hour during which they monitor you. I had to have 20 ECT treatments, about two treatments per week, from the beginning of October of 2014 to the end of December 2014. I can't remember a whole lot surrounding the time of the treatments, nor can I remember some things even from years ago, and I still have trouble recalling things. I continued in telling my questioning friend that I did not mean to sound completely negative about ECT or my experience with it. I advised her that if she was extremely desperate, such as I was back then, that she might, indeed want to consider doing it. I do think it helped me. It just took a long while after the treatments for me to recognize how much it did help. For at least a year afterwards, I swore I would never ever have ECT done to me again, but Katie reminds me of how very bad I was, depression wise, and I knew I had to do it and just hoped that it would help me.

I was not permitted to drive for about three months during the treatments and for some time afterwards. My last ECT treatment was on December 22, 2014, and I considered it the greatest Christmas present of all time. I was so happy and thrilled to be getting my very last treatment that beforehand, I strolled into that nurse's room for my final assessment, sat down at the testing table and jokingly said, "truck, flower, red, three, dog. There. Can I go home now?" before the nurse could even ask me a question. It made the nurse laugh as she knew how very eager I was to be done with the treatments.

I had to add, in replying to my friend asking about my ECT experience, because I wanted to be completely honest about it with her, that getting the treatments didn't really help with my depression. At least they did not help right away, and it really fucked with my short and long-term memory. The short-term memories eventually improved somewhat, but there are still huge events from my long-term memory of which I have absolutely no recollection. This has been, and still is to this day, very upsetting to me. Katie and my Mom will say that the treatments saved my life, and essentially, they did. It was at least an entire year after I was completely done with all the treatments, however, that I was glad that I had agreed to getting them.

I was glad to be putting this horrible experience behind me…. but was I better? Well, the ECT treatments shocked the mania and racing thoughts out of me. I honestly felt mildly retarded. I'm not using that word to be disrespectful or to joke about it. I am very serious. My thoughts were so slowed down that I had trouble even forming complete thoughts. I noticed that my brain took a lot longer to process things, too. When someone would ask me something, I felt like a long time would pass before I understood what they said to me, process it in my brain, and was able to respond back to them. This must have been exaggerated somewhat in my mind because people would tell me that it didn't really take as long as I felt like it did before I could respond back to them. I know that my brain took longer to digest and hear things, though. I couldn't think quick on my feet, like I was able to do before the treatments. It took me longer to understand things like concepts, too. It felt like it took me longer to organize my thoughts to where I could have them make sense when I spoke. Eventually, my short-term memory got a little better. I could finally remember how to drive to my parent's house, which was only an easy, 30-minute drive from my house, and a drive that I have made thousands of times before.

My long-term memory started to come back a little bit, but to this day it's not the same. There are so many things surrounding my hospital stay, the ECT treatments, and even memories of years and years before all of this that I just can't make my brain recall. There are large parts of my life that are just gone, maybe forever. I'm talking about recent and past vacations that I went on with my mom. I can't even create a picture in my mind of these things. It's like those vacations never happened. I am still grieving over the loss of my memory that was damaged. So, was it worth it? Am I glad that I went through with the ECT treatments? First, I must say that it wasn't a cure all, magic fix that made everything better. Thankfully, they didn't present it as such when I first went in. When I hear my loved ones tell me how extremely depressed I was before I went into the hospital and how they tell me that I was so much better after the treatments, I guess I have to say that I am glad that I went through with it. It really felt like my only option, other than to carry out my resignation to my life. I just must trust and believe my loved ones when they tell me that I am so much better than I was before. They all tell me that the ECT treatments "saved my life," but if you asked me if I would ever go through it again, I'm sorry, but the answer more than likely would be NO. I never want to ever go through anything like that again, and I just hope that I am never in a place in my life where that would be my only option.

Directly after the treatments my depression wasn't completely gone, but I was on better footing to deal with it in therapy. My thoughts eventually, slowly got to a place where they felt more normal in their arrival and response time and I slowly became able to grasp concepts a little better. Can you believe that I missed my mania and racing thoughts? Of course, I did something called "romanticizing the past" with missing the mania, which means I remembered the mania as wonderful and good. I liked feeling energized by my mania. I liked being able to multi-task and get stuff done. I liked feeling so very high. But with romanticizing the past, you don't remember it how it truly was, and I wasn't remembering how horrible the racing thoughts were when they were happening. It was like I couldn't keep up with my thoughts and they would come so very fast, overwhelming me to the point where I really couldn't function or keep my thoughts straight/in order or make sense out of them. I didn't recall how the mania would be so intense that it would make me think irrationally, make me have delusional thoughts, and think I could do things that were not humanly possible, like jumping off that bridge and surviving it. So, when I remember how my manic side truly was, I guess I can say that I don't miss everything about the mania. Most of it was quite dangerous, I suppose. But, even though they warned me that the ECT wasn't anything magical that would take my bipolar disorder away completely, I still was disappointed when it didn't. I just would think after all that I went through with it, I expected to not have to struggle with my mood, at least for some time. It took at least a year for my brain to heal from the trauma it experienced from the shock treatments, for the medicine to start really making a difference in my mood, and for me to feel somewhat normal again.

Every person's experience with it is probably a little or maybe a lot different, but for me, it was truly the most frightening thing I had ever gone through. So, with those details being said, you ask, would I recommend it? Yes, if it was your last resort. I am thankfully on the right medication and dosage now, so my mood has been good for quite some time, and I am truly grateful for that. It's an amazing feeling to just feel and be "happy" with no hint of depression. Now, I know I am not "cured." That's just not how bipolar disorder works, but I certainly am enjoying feeling pleasant without that cloud of depression hanging over my head. I still get bad days, bad moods, and get sad, but it's nothing like the intensity of a mood that insists the answer to ending your mental pain is to end it **all**.

I must reemphasize, ECT treatments are not a cure-all. The intent of it is to disrupt brain patterns in such a way that medication can be effective again. It's a shock to the system, for sure, but that is the purpose. My medications that I was taking for my bipolar disorder, before the ECT had to be done, worked for a very long time, until they stopped working. Unfortunately, that is something that sometimes can happen with medications for mental illnesses, in that they can work for a period of time, and then somehow either your brain gets used to them, or something changes in the brain, and the medications simply stop being effective. Sometimes, when this happens, a different medication can be tried, or the medication you are currently taking can be increased and that will help. Sometimes a medication can be added, in addition to what you are already taking. And then there are sometimes, even after trying these things, the changes don't help to alleviate the symptoms and then more drastic measures like ECT must be considered. The good news is that this isn't always true for every person who is taking a medication for his or her mental illness. Sometimes the medication a person takes for their condition rarely needs adjusted or changed, but unfortunately for me, that ended up not being the case. For me, I ended up finding myself in the psychiatric hospital getting the electroconvulsive therapy. That's where I was finding myself back in 2014, but here it is, 2017, and I am still in the process of finding myself.

Therefore, I am not titling this book "*Found Herself There.*" There really is no end destination for finding oneself. It's like the difference between survived and surviving, in that it's more about

finding than being found. Or as they say, it's more about the journey than the destination. As for me, I got to a place where I not only found myself, but accepted myself as well. However, I knew that it was only a stop on the journey. Respite does feel good, though. Finding yourself in a good place feels quite wonderful, in fact. It doesn't feel manically amazing, it's just a sense of knowing that it's okay to stop, to take a breath, to look around and even to like what you see, sometimes. As of the beginning of 2016 and to this day, I am still thoroughly enjoying that much needed respite, however long it will last this time.

During this time of feeling completely free of depression, I decided it was important to write a personal letter to my "depressed self," while I am feeling so good and symptom free. I did this because I know that my depressed self could start to come back at any time and when I am in that intense depressed state, I know that I cannot recall a time when I ever felt even remotely good. When a severe depression hits, everything turns black and I would swear that I never had a good day in my life, where I wasn't depressed. I can't remember the good times, the happy, healthy times of being symptom free when the dark clouds start to take over. So, I felt it was important for my healthy self, the self I am right now, to write my future depressed self a letter. Depression tells your brain lies, and when everything turns dark to where you can't see reality clearly, it's important to remind yourself that there is another side from which you will come out, given time. I wanted to include this letter that I wrote to my depressed self in this book to give you an example of a letter you could write to your own self, too. If you have bipolar disorder, depression, or another mental health disorder that's applicable to this, I recommend picking a time when you are happy, mentally healthy and feeling good. Then, write a loving, compassionate, personal letter to your future depressed self for you to read when your own depression rears its ugly head again. It's no guarantee, but it might help you in the future. I share with you my personal letter to my depressed self now, as an example:

Dear depressed self,

First, let me say that I know you are hurting and are in pain. You know that I have been there with you in the deepest and darkest of times. I remember that during these times I thought our thinking was crystal clear and made perfect sense, but honestly, it is our mental illness that makes us believe that lie. I know that it feels very real to you. I know how ending our life seems like the only solution to our intense pain and suffering. It doesn't just feel like the only solution, but the right solution, as well. But, I am here now, as your healthy self, to tell you that it is NOT the right solution, nor the only solution. You will try to argue with me about challenging the reality that you feel right now, but your extremely negative beliefs about life right now are NOT your true reality. However, at this point, it is not helpful to debate whether the reality you feel now is the TRUTH versus the more positive reality that I feel now (as I write this to you as my healthy self). Just because your feelings and thoughts SEEM real or true, does NOT mean that they ARE real and true. We can allow these thoughts and feelings to GO, just as they came. We do not have to attach ourselves to them or make them our true beliefs.

*One of the greatest lessons you learned from your mentor, Debbie, was that **IT WILL PASS**. I know that RIGHT NOW it doesn't FEEL like it ever will pass, but it will, if you stay strong enough to stick it out and get through it. I remember the exhaustion of depression and the feeling of being so overwhelmed that you just cannot take it anymore. It's at this time you need to DISTRACT yourself from your thoughts and emotions by using the many coping skills and distraction techniques you have learned over the years. Take a nap, if you can. Write down and journal your thoughts/*

feelings onto paper to get them OUT of your head. Draw, paint, etc., and create whatever you are feeling/thinking into a form of art as a way of expression. Look at your coping skills list.

Lastly, remember that you have loved ones who would be devastated if you chose to end your life. I know you are suffering, but you are not that cruel. If you can't live for yourself right now, do it for them. Do it for your Mom, for Katie, for everyone you love. Good feelings do not last, but bad feelings do NOT last, either. This is the ebb and flow of life. Accepting that life is not fair is very hard, I know, but you can still be helpful to others, once you are through this. YOU WILL GET THROUGH THIS IF YOU STAY STRONG. Look at the phoenix that is forever tattooed on your arm. YOU WILL RISE ABOVE THIS. IT WILL PASS. YOU WILL BE ABLE TO HELP OTHERS AND ENCOURAGE THEM through this life and that is what you believe the purpose of life is all about: Loving others and helping them through this life, as well.

So, I am not asking you to deny what you are feeling. FEEL THE FEELINGS. THINK THE THOUGHTS. But, then let them GO. Please keep us safe, Melissa, until you can feel well again. And if all else fails, please use the crisis intervention plan, reach out for help to keep us alive at all costs. This healthy self of ours who is writing to you right now is still with you. I am in there, under the dirt and mud, and you are not alone. You can do this. I love and believe in you.

With respect and admiration,
Your healthy self

UNFORTUNATELY, WITH ECT YOU DON'T GET TO CHOOSE THE MEMORIES YOU WOULD LIKE TO FORGET VS. THE ONES THAT RESURFACE THAT YOU DON'T WANT TO REMEMBER

It's odd how the ECT stole much of my memory and my ability to recall things, but at the same time, it also brought some things to the surface that were buried deep within my mind. Naturally these things were not memories of which I was thrilled to be reminded. They weren't events from my past that I had totally forgotten, just ones that I really thought I dealt with, at least for the most part, and thought I had healed from. The devil truly is in the details though, and those damn details needed dealt with now because they were fully to the surface and in my face. For example, a significant, horrifying event from my past was the rape that happened to me when I was a teenager, by my boyfriend, who I thought loved me, who I thought I could trust, and who I never thought would do something like that to me.

Granted, I didn't deal with this trauma, at least not in the proper ways, for a very long time after it happened. It took me a long enough time to tell anyone else what happened at that time because one of the two people I was brave enough to tell immediately told me "that was just how men were and that I should pray for him." Of course, with that kind of response from an adult whom I looked up to and trusted with, as to what happened to me, it wasn't really encouraging to reveal it to anyone else. When I look back on this person's reaction, it does make sense why she would tell me that. She was the submissive wife of the head of a small religious cult, of which I was a mesmerized member. It really wasn't the response I needed to hear, though. It wasn't a normal response and it just made me feel a lot shittier about the whole thing. So, I "dealt" with the trauma of the rape in very self-destructive ways for a long time, before I came to a point in my life where I could deal with it effectively, correctly, and more appropriately, to heal from it.

Years later, after almost near self-destruction, I started seriously dealing with the rape in therapy and confronted those demons. I even wrote about the rape in my first book and doing that was very healing. I just wanted other victims to know that it's important to deal with trauma like this. It's important to not only deal with it, but to allow yourself to feel it, and then eventually heal from it. That first answer/remark I received back at that time from the wife of the cult leader was, I suppose, somewhat understandable from her point of view, but was also false. I refused to accept that that was just the way men were (all rapists?), and that the thing I needed to do was to pray for the soul of my boyfriend who committed the crime of rape against me. After working hard with various therapists, processing the rape, I did think I was healed and could move on.

There were many thoughts and feelings that I still had about the rape that festered within me, though. I still considered my teenage inner self to be "stupid" for not seeing the signs that my boyfriend previously showed, that might have indicated that he would do this to me. I have tremendous guilt that I didn't tell my mother and other people about the crime when it happened, so that he would be held accountable for it. Maybe even preventing him from raping someone else in the future, because if that did happen, I feel it would be my fault since I did not report the crime. At that time, back then, I was terrified of telling anyone, though. I didn't recognize the rape as a crime. I didn't realize that it was more about power and control rather than sex. And I knew if I told my mother what had just happened to me, it would devastate her. I never wanted to hurt my mother or allow her to be hurt. I guess I was also afraid that no one would believe me. I don't know why I felt that way, but I knew that if I would have been able to get past the shame and humiliation of it all and tell someone, only to have them question the validity of it happening, for whatever reason, I knew that would destroy me completely. That would have finished that job of killing me. When I finally did reveal it to my therapist, years after it happened, she DID believe me. She educated me on what rape was really about and she tried her best to help me deal with the haunting, torturing negative emotions, thoughts and feelings I still had about being raped.

I used to think that the worst part about the rape, aside from the shattered trust I had given to a person who I sincerely thought loved me, was the fact that I felt that I could no longer even trust myself, my gut instinct, because how did I not see that this was going to happen? But, the worst part about the actual rape itself while it was happening was how terrified I felt, how in shock I was that it was happening, how panic-stricken I was, how I just wanted to be dead because I couldn't stop it from happening. I felt completely subdued, trapped, powerless, helpless, and since he was pushing his huge hand down on my face to try and prevent me from screaming, it was covering my nose and mouth as well, and I seriously felt like I couldn't even breathe. I went away in my mind because I couldn't handle what was happening to me, what he was doing to me. I felt so small. My voice meant nothing. My struggling, my attempts at pleading with him meant nothing, like I was a piece of garbage or just an object that was being used. I used to wish he would have just killed me. It definitely helped to finally talk to a therapist about the rape, though.

However, I only focused on what I referred to as "the main event," the rape itself. I minimized and avoided talking about the other abuse I suffered the entire two years that I was with this man prior to the rape. I avoided it for several reasons. First, I was very ashamed to talk about it because those two years of sexual, mental, verbal, and emotional abuse that I endured should have been huge red flags that the "main event" was eventually going to happen to me by him. I felt stupid that I didn't see these warning signs and therefore it made me feel even more like the rape was my fault and that I allowed it to happen to me.

I changed after the rape. A part of me did die. I couldn't trust or feel safe anymore. I believed I was only that object to be used by other people. My needs and wants meant nothing. I no longer felt heard. I did not matter. I hated myself, blamed myself, and was so very angry and afraid at the same time. But, the very worst part about the whole thing now is that, in a way, I am not a *survivor* of rape. I'm still a *victim* of rape, because it still has control over my life. I am still controlled, still feel that same powerless feeling, and that's what angers me the most. I can't seem to get an entire grip on my life because now, after the ECT treatments, I get so very easily triggered, so easily violated, and I never want to be vulnerable like that again. I allowed myself to be defined as I was treated. I viewed myself as garbage, or an object to be abused, because that was how I was treated. How you are treated, however, says more about the person abusing you rather than about you, yourself. Just because you are treated like trash does not mean you are trash. Yet, after this happened to me, I did see myself as how he defined me. l already had low self-esteem to begin with and by being treated this way by someone who I trusted and thought loved me, it stuck in my head somehow that I deserved to be treated badly from there on out. I hated myself and found myself in many unhealthy relationships throughout my life after that because I didn't believe that I deserved better.

After years and years of working on myself in therapy to develop a better self-esteem and a more accurate belief about myself, I slowly started to choose healthier partners with the occasional "what the hell was I thinking with that one?" thrown in occasionally when my self- esteem would backslide. But, honestly, it wasn't until I truly believed that I deserved better, that I received better. I got better, in fact, I got the best, when I met my life partner who I am with now (and KNOW that I truly will be with for life), Katie. She is truly my soulmate and the person who my spirit had been searching for my entire life. I love her so deeply and so much and I feel the same deep love back from her. I am so very grateful and appreciative to have her as my partner and best friend. We have been together almost 6 years now, since November 20, 2011, and I am happy to say that this search in my life is complete. My heart has found its home. Katie is my home.

As a teenager, I would have never even dreamt that the love I have with Katie could even exist, let alone believe that I could ever deserve someone like her. Back then, I was treated like trash, so that's what I thought I was. As a teen, I didn't realize that when someone treats you like trash, it doesn't mean that you are trash, it means that they are trash. Back then, I didn't understand this. I was only a young teen when I started dating "James." He was my first official boyfriend and was 4 years older than me. During the two years I was dating him, I endured some very intense abuse. I guess I didn't recognize it as abuse, or didn't want to see it as abuse, but that's what it was. Even though I was young, I feel as though I should have seen the warning signs. For instance, when he grabbed me by the throat, squeezing off my airway till I couldn't breathe while holding that tight grasp for what seemed like forever, reminding me that he could kill me if he wanted to, before finally releasing his grip, was not a normal thing a loving boyfriend did to his girlfriend. I felt stupid for not knowing this, not realizing this then. I did not tell a single soul about the entire two years this all was happening, and I never told anyone up until the ECT brought it all raw and to the surface, to where I knew I had to deal with it to heal from it. I then told exactly two people. I told Katie, and I told my therapist, who I had been seeing for a long time. A couple of weeks after I revealed this shameful, intense, secret that was keeping me sick, to my therapist, she abruptly left the center where I was seeing her for therapy. This was unrelated, of course, but it was very painful, nonetheless. It triggered my issues with abandonment. I had shared something with someone, so personal, so hard to talk about, so embarrassing to admit, only to have her suddenly abandon me, leaving me feeling cold, naked, and exposed.

They say that sometimes bad or unpleasant things happen to you so that better, good things can happen and I feel this was the case with my former therapist leaving the center. The new therapist I got happens to specialize in and is trained in trauma therapy. So, I am on the road to healing those secrets with her to put them in their proper place in my mind. I have really been struggling with PTSD (post-traumatic stress disorder) symptoms since the upheaval of the sexual abuse, and it's very hard to deal with at times.

My current therapist is teaching me more about post-traumatic stress disorder. There was a time when people thought the only people suffering from PTSD were soldiers who have come home from war. However, psychiatrists, doctors, and therapists are now realizing that trauma comes in many different shapes and sizes. Trauma includes things like loss of a loved one, all forms of abuse, such as sexual, emotional, verbal, mental, as well as physical abuse, terrifying accidents such as car wrecks, and basically any intense event that seems to "scar you" on the inside, that sticks with you for weeks, months, even many years after the event happened. The event doesn't even have to happen to you personally. PTSD can occur in someone who even *witnessed* a terrible event. Some research states that there are three main categories used to determine PTSD. The following information has been gathered from The Anxiety and Depression Association of America website[5].

These three paraphrased categories of symptoms are:

1. Reliving or re-experiencing the traumatic event through distressful, intrusive memories, such as flashbacks, triggers, and/or nightmares about the traumatic event.
2. Avoidance of activities, places, people that remind the victim of the traumatic event; includes a feeling of emotional numbness.
3. Hypersensitivity, hypervigilance, such as being easily angered, agitated, irritated, with increased arousal with things like difficulty concentrating and problems with sleeping. The victim often feels "on edge" with great anxiety.

More symptoms from these three categories include:

*   Nightmares
*   Disturbing recollections of event, often spontaneous in occurrence
*   Flashbacks or other reactions where the victim will dissociate are described as the victim
*   feeling like she/he is reliving the traumatic event
*   Sensitivity and distress at exposure to things that symbolize and remind the victim of the
*   traumatic event
*   Physiological reactions to reminders of traumatic event
*   Intrusive, distressing memories of traumatic event where the victim wants to avoid these
*   reminders

- Exaggerated negative beliefs about self and the world
- Distorted blame of self or others as to the cause of the traumatic event
- Persistent fear, terror, anxiety, irritability, anger, guilt, shame, feelings of detachment, a lack of interest in being around other people, reckless, even self-destructive behavior
- The inability to experience positive emotions, and a feeling like the victim is on high alert
- Also, victims experience triggers which are defined as anything from an event, a person, a sound, even a smell that so strongly reminds the victim of the trauma that he/she feels as though she/he is experiencing the trauma over again. Triggers can vary in intensity from small reminders (consciously and subconsciously) that will make the victim feel extremely uncomfortable to a full-blown trigger where the victim dissociates and feels as though he/she is back, re-experiencing the trauma all over again
- Triggers can often set off major panic attacks, as well

These are just some of the main symptoms that I have learned that are associated with PTSD. There are other symptoms not included here and a vast amount of research, studies, and information that can be found online for those who want to learn even more about post-traumatic stress disorder. My symptoms usually come in the form of feeling extremely hypervigilant, that feeling of always having to be "on guard" for something terrible to happen. I experience an almost constant state of some level of anxiety. I don't sleep well or soundly at night and am a very light sleeper. For the last year or so, I cannot even sleep upstairs, in my bed, next to my partner, because I must sleep on the couch in the living room so that I can hear the front door if someone tries to break in. I feel I wouldn't be able to hear from upstairs if someone was trying to get into the house, so every night I sleep downstairs. I check and recheck the locks on the doors many times throughout the day and evening. I have boundary issues, especially with males. I have trust issues. I am highly reactive to sudden sounds, etc. And I experience triggers when I see, hear, or just even feel something that directly reminds me of the sexual trauma that I experienced over 29 years ago. Some of these triggers I am aware of and have come to understand why they are triggers to me. Yet, there are still things that happen, things I see, hear, taste, touch, smell, experience, that trigger me and I do not understand why or how they are related to my trauma.

I think there are many people who simply do not understand what it is truly like to have PTSD. They think people who suffer with this affliction simply won't *let go of the past*, but it's actually the *past* that won't *let go* of us. We think and feel differently than people who do not have PTSD. We tend to be more sensitive to our surroundings and more affected by other people in general. We own a little piece of paranoia and can't fully relax like other people can. Please be patient with people who have PTSD (or any other mental disorder). You can't see our illness on the outside, but if you take the time to listen, you might be able to see the fear in our eyes that is with us daily, causing us the anxiety, that you have a tough time understanding. They say perception is reality, and that everyone's perception is a little (or a lot) different. With people who have PTSD, their perception is tainted by past trauma and we really do not see or experience things the same way. I highly recommend people to learn more about PTSD, especially if you have a loved one who suffers from it. It might make their reactions to things make a little more sense to you.

I am still in the process of learning about PTSD and my own trauma, as it affects my life. I am working hard with my new therapist to work through the trauma because I know that is the only way I am going to heal and move on from it. It's true that "the only way out is through." And I am a strong believer in the importance of feeling it to deal with it, and eventually heal from it. Someday I will see myself fully as a survivor of it and not just a victim. There's a popular saying by Akshay Dubey, that I included in my first book that states, "*Healing doesn't mean the damage never existed. It means the damage no longer controls your life.*"[6] But I have come to realize that healing is not a onetime thing. It's not linear, but circular and ongoing, just like the journey of finding yourself. As you heal each of your psychological wounds, I believe the damage controls you less and less. However, since the journey is never ending, neither is the healing.

IN THEIR FEET
(a poem by Melissa Ross)

People will think what they sometimes think,
And into depression, I sometimes sink,

Wondering why God made me this way,
Left-handed, bipolar, brown haired and gay.

We don't always choose the moods we are in,
In battling ourselves, we don't always win.

But, please don't ever say or think we don't try,
Not all of us find relief when looking to the sky.

It's not that we don't believe or want to take your advice,
And we know that you care and are just trying to be nice.

We each have our own journeys,
though, and roads of our own,
Your path for me won't work, no
matter the light that's shown.

Just please be patient, while we each find our way,
Not behind or in front, but beside us, every day.

For we are all around you, no matter what you think,
Each of us are so different, but connected by a link.

If we are not you, or at least someone you know,
You will encounter us some day, in this life's long show.

SO, who am I talking about here?
To whom am I referring?
The lines are getting crossed now and
your reality is suddenly blurring.

I'm just saying be gentle to each fragile soul you meet,
You don't know what they're going through,
unless you're standing in their feet.

ALGEBRA SUCKED IN HIGH SCHOOL, BUT IT DOES MAKE SENSE WHEN YOU USE IT IN PSYCHOLOGY

Previously, before getting the new therapist who is trained in PTSD, I was being honest in therapy, doing my homework, and practicing throughout the week the new way of thinking that I was learning from my therapist, which was: "I think, therefore I feel." It was a challengingly new way of looking at my thinking, though, because I was (and partly still am, but don't tell my therapist who left me) a firm believer in the belief that emotions cause thoughts, not the other way around. So, it was a new approach, the whole "I feel_____ because I thought _____" notion.

I had learned that with the A+B=C psychological model, that it's in fact, not A that causes C, but B that causes C. Let me explain. A is the activating event, B is the belief you have about that event, and C is the consequence or end result of how you feel about the event. On the surface, you'd think that it was the event that causes you to feel what you feel about it after it's over, but that's not always true. It's the belief you attach to the event that causes you to think/feel what you think and/or feel about what happened. I like to give this scenario as an example.

Say you are driving down the road in your car and it's wet and muddy outside. A big tractor trailer truck comes at you on their side of the road and as it passes you, it splashes up a bunch of ugly, wet rain on your windshield. Your immediate thought could be, "Damn truck made my window all messy and I can't see out of it now! This day keeps getting shittier!" And then you are in an even worse mood than before. You'd say that the event of the truck splashing the dirty rain on your windshield caused you feel or believe what you believed about it, right? However, (and this really happened to me this way, that's why I like to use it as an example), what if you were out of wiper fluid and your windshield was already so muddy that you could hardly see out of it and you were dreading having to pull over and stop to put more wiper fluid in your car and you weren't even sure if you had a jug of it in your trunk. THEN, the truck comes by, splashing the dirty water on your windshield, but it wets your windshield just enough that you then can use your wipers and clear your already muddy windshield. When this happened to me I thought, "Wow! I'm glad that truck went by me, splashing that water on my windshield because now I can clear my window with my wipers, since I was out of windshield wiper fluid! That worked out great!" And then I had a better attitude about what the rest of my day was going to be like. In this example, it's not really A. (the event) that caused C. (the attitude I had directly after it happened), but it was B. (my belief or how I viewed what happened with the truck passing me by like that) that truly caused C. (my attitude about what the rest of my day was going to be like from there on out). Maybe this is a stupid example and harder to understand than I think it is, but it often really is the thoughts and feelings we attach to life events that determine our attitude/mood or consequential result.

Another magical algebraic equation that I learned is that $S = P \times R$. Pain times resistance equals suffering. Suffering drives and distorts. It prolongs pain. The more I would not let myself feel my emotional/mental pain, the more I felt it. The more I resisted dealing with things or resisted the grief process, the more I suffered. I learned that if I do not resist the pain and just let myself feel it, let myself grieve, and let myself work through the pain, this will cut the amount of my suffering time down immensely. Yes, it hurts, but as I paraphrase what my mentor, Debbie, told me, "Any kind of growth and progress is going to hurt, as if they are growing pains of the mind and soul." And just as the stone that she gave me that still sits on my desk to this day reads: "It will pass." (The joke is to add the part that, *it might pass like a kidney stone, but it will pass!*) I learned that bad thoughts and feelings do not last if we do not attach ourselves to them. If we don't hold onto them, they eventually do pass. I just need to wait them out. That little stone and what she wrote on it has gotten me through some very desperate times when I thought an intensely negative feeling, like depression, would last forever. But, indeed, the bad thought or painfully negative feeling DID pass, just like the giver of that stone said it eventually would. It's true that "the only way out is through." We can't just be expected to "get over" things. I'll say it again, we must *deal to heal*. The whole notion of suffering being pain that is met with resistance reminds me of the quote by Haruki Murakami that reads, "Pain is inevitable. Suffering is optional." Knowing the difference between pain and suffering is the key. Suffering is the distressful experience of going through the emotional or physical pain. If we allow ourselves to go through the pain without resistance, we get through it quicker to the other side of it.

I was never one to tolerate distress very well. It is a characteristic of my bipolar disorder. However, through much work in therapy, I am learning distress tolerance, which is part of (DBT) dialectical behavioral therapy. I have learned things called *crisis survival strategies*, which include: self-soothing techniques, improving the moment, and thinking of the pros and cons. This training has taught me to decrease negative behaviors that cause me grief and torment. It also taught me to increase the behaviors that help me feel better, like the skills of interpersonal effectiveness, emotional regulation, and core mindfulness, to name a few.

Some people might accuse me of not carrying around that *half full* glass. These people have blamed that from the beginning and they quite frustrate me. Ever since I read about a more suitable look for me to the theory of the glass being half full or half empty, I have been quite satisfied with saying I wasn't an optimist or a pessimist, but an opportunist, and just drank whatever was in the glass. I was fortunate enough to be seeing a therapist at the time who didn't insist on me seeing the glass as half full, and this helped me greatly. She didn't ask me to look on the bright side. She was teaching me how to look on the realistic side, and that made much more sense to me than trying to "fake it until I make it." She wasn't forcing me to read daily affirmations about how things could be way worse, either. She was a cognitive behavioral therapist who, like I said, was trying to teach me that my thoughts are the cause my emotions, and I struggled with this as a hard lesson to learn, but I was trying to learn it, trying to fully believe it. However, prior to the ECT treatments, my mood still started crashing downward again. I was feeling shitty again. I was feeling depressed again. So I had to ask myself, "What was I thinking that was causing these emotions!? This is somehow my fault." I expressed this shame to my therapist and I was so thankful when she said that with mental illness, the thoughts are not always a choice. This helped me to not feel so flawed, so weak-minded, so guilt-ridden with the belief that I just wasn't trying hard enough in therapy. She assured me that I was putting the work and dedication into therapy, but for some reason, my medication started not working so well.

Unfortunately, this can really happen. You can be walking along your path fine and then discover the ground is quicksand again. And that's exactly what happened to me. It became figuratively harder to walk, harder to make my legs move through the denseness of the increasingly thick sand around them. The unwanted, uninvited thoughts became worse as things darkened around me in my mind. I know some of you know how extremely frustrating this is. For those of you who don't, please just trust me that it is extremely devastating when you have to start to admit that things are getting out of your control again, and that there's very little you can do about it. The things that I could do be doing to help me get out of my depressive episode, I was doing them, the opportunist. Nowadays, I describe myself more as a realist with hope, and I am just glad that the glass is refillable.

I LOVE YOU, SO I'LL EAT YOU LAST

**(a short essay written as an example of
the stupid shit that I worry about)**

If you don't want to challenge your thinking, put down this book. If you live in a figurative box and want to stay there, stop reading. If you believe that Jesus is the only way to "Heaven," burn this book and run screaming to your nearest church. If you don't want to *wonder* and possibly get lost, this book is not for you. If I have offended thee in any way, read no further. It's only going to get worse. If all the above is true and you are still reading, good. Keep reading. Maybe you are ready. Lastly, if you think this chapter is going to be entirely about cannibalism, you will be greatly disappointed. And I must add that if you don't like people telling you what to do, don't read this book! (That's my little reverse psychology joke).

With all that being said, considering the anxiety condition that I have, I worry about stupid things. I worry about things that 87% of the time are not going to happen and aren't even likely to happen. I dwell. I obsess. I worry about crazy things. For example, I've never really been afraid of flying, per se. I've just been afraid of crashing. Luckily, I don't have to travel by airplane very often, actually not at all. I have had to use air travel, however, when I would go on vacations with my mom in my past. After everyone has boarded, crammed into their seats, decided if they want the "free to pee" seat or the scenic view, the flight attendant starts his or her hand signals while the recording tells us what to do if the plan goes down... "put your air mask on first, and then assist others," I start to think. Maybe I have seen too many plane crash movies where the plane goes down in this remote area and there are survivors, but there's very little chance of being rescued. After all the mini bags of pretzels are gone, they have to resort to cannibalism. This is what I think about each time I would be sitting on a plane and it's about to take off. I look around. Who would I eat first? You might think this is a very distasteful thought, pun intended, but I'm a realist and it's a good distraction from the pain that comes from my ears popping from the air pressure.

Now, I'd like to say, "Well, I'd choose to just starve. I'd refuse to actually eat human flesh." But, then I remembered how hungry I get every day by supper time, and I rethink it. I'm just being honest. They always say that you don't really know what you would do in a situation until you are in it, so maybe that's true for resorting to cannibalism to stay alive if the plane goes down. I mean, I also think that I could never kill anyone, even in self-defense. But, then I think about a murderer breaking into my house and threatening to hurt Katie or our cats, and I decide that yes, I could probably seriously hurt someone, if I had to do so. So, that's what I think about when I am on an airplane. Who would I eat first? We've already discussed the absolute horror of being in a situation like this and having to decide, so I think further. Surely, we surviving passengers would agree to eat the dead first. I mean, if you think about it, the bodies of the passengers who died when the plane crashed are really just dead carcasses. Their soul isn't there any longer, right? It's either in Heaven or Hell or whatever you believe in, but the bodies are just fleshy meat, right? Sure, it would be harder if you knew the expired person whose body you had to eat as sustenance to live, but what are the odds of that? But, after the dead bodies have all been eaten and we are on day 30 of no food, would my eyes fall upon the oldest of the lot because they have lived a long life, or would I not be able to digest such flesh because it's old and wrinkly? A baby's flesh would probably be the most tender, but who in the world could go there? You surely would start with strangers first and not your beloved travel companions. But, what if it came down to that? What if all the strangers were eaten by day 60 of being stranded out in some freezing cold wintery mountain top or in some blistering desert? What if it came down to just you and your loved one with whom you were traveling? Who would eat who? Maybe this concern, this fear, this situational problem, is unrealistic and you have never ever thought you'd have to worry about such a thing, but this is an example of the extreme things some people with anxiety disorder worry about. I am sure that the rugby players who got stranded after their plane crashed and had to resort to cannibalism to stay alive probably thought they'd never have to worry about such a thing, either. I mean, the movie based on this true event is called, *"Alive"* and that's how they stayed alive was by eating the other passengers aboard the flight. This image haunts me each time I do choose to travel by airplane. I cram into my seat aboard the plane with the other passengers, strap myself in, look to my friend or family member who is traveling with me and I think to myself, "I love you, so I'll eat you last."

WE ALL ARE THE CHEESE AND THE CHEESE STANDS ALONE

Some readers might wonder why I have included that last chapter. It wasn't really about cannibalism, but more about how, in the end, all we have is ourselves. That is one reason why it's so important to learn to love yourself along your journey to finding yourself, because you are going to be with you for the rest of your life. Another important message of that essay is the fact that we really must put our own air masks on first, before we help others, just like the flight attendant tells you when you board any plane. There's a saying that you can't pour from an empty cup, and it's true. If you don't first take care of yourself, you can be no good to or for someone else. If you don't know how you deserve to be treated, or if you treat yourself badly, the people you surround yourself with, especially in a romantic relationship, are going to take note of how you treat yourself and treat you accordingly. If you don't love yourself first, how are others going to love you? If you don't think you are lovable, how are you going to expect others to love you? If you don't value yourself, how are others going to see your worth? If you want to call it selfishness, fine, although I do not agree that a person is being selfish by putting her/himself first, taking care of her/himself first, before trying to care for and love another. You must have love within you to have love to give outwardly. If you need to look at it this way, it's actually cruel to be with someone else when you haven't worked on your own self first, gotten your own "ducks in a row" as best you can, or aren't at least in the active process of trying to be the best version of yourself you can be, because it's not fair to the other person. You are bringing a damaged self into a relationship with someone else and they are going to have to deal with that if you don't do it first, or if you aren't actively working on it.

No one should have to or feel like they have to save you. You must save yourself. And you also cannot save another person, no matter how badly you want to save them from hurt, from harm, from terribly bad choices, from disaster, from self-destruction, from any of it. All you can do is love them. We can assist others on their journeys to heal themselves, but we cannot do it for them. We can't walk their walk or make them walk faster. And we can't force them to do it for themselves when they aren't ready. It's their journey, no matter how very painful it is for you to watch them stumble and fall and even get burned. They must live it to learn it. We also shouldn't set ourselves on fire to keep another person warm. We are all the cheese and the cheese stands alone in the end, and on the journey to finding oneself.

Thinking back to the plane crash scenario, you probably would eat a loved one, if that was what you had to do to stay alive. Whether you want to believe right now that you would do such a horrific act, no one truly knows what they would do until they are actually in the situation, especially faced with the severity of death of self. Most of us, probably all of us, really, have a built-in mechanism called self-preservation. This is where, when it comes right down to it, we will do whatever we must do to survive. Some people's self-preservation mechanism inside them has been damaged, though. These are the people you see who are always putting other people's wants and needs above their own. These people will drown themselves to try to save another from drowning. Some of these people value themselves so very little, or not at all, that they never even consider their wants or needs, even the need to stay healthy and alive, because they were trained not to, somewhere along the line, probably stemming from childhood. We can debate nature vs. nurture and whether they were born that way, or have been taught this from their parents, guardians, or society in general, but the end result is the same. This damaged self-preservation mechanism in these particular people must be repaired and healed, or at least be in the process thereof, before they should get into a relationship with another person.

I hear couples who are in love often say that they complete each other. While a statement like, "She completes me" seems like a term of endearment on the surface, a total commitment to being in love with the other person, I shudder when I hear it being said. I used to say the same thing about some of the people whom I have loved and with whom I was in romantic relationships. However, I strongly believe now that we must first be complete by our own selves. We can't look for another to complete us because, again, that's not fair to the other person. He/she has enough to do with completing their own self. When two people who are entirely whole on their own get together, I believe there is a higher rate of them staying together. Like I said before, it's not fair to bring your damaged, incomplete self into a relationship, unless you are working on your own to complete yourself at the same time. When someone who is with someone who "completes" them ends up losing the person for whatever reason, it's only natural that they are going to feel incomplete again because they don't have that part of the other person to get nourishment from to feel whole. To complete someone seems romantic, but it's a recipe for problems in the relationship.

I no longer say that someone completes me. With Katie, I say that she doesn't complete me, she enhances me. I was already complete when we got together and she enhances me by helping to bring out the very best in me. She makes me want to continue each day to strive to be a better person than I was the day before. Even to call someone your other half indicates that you aren't whole by yourself. People who are only a half of themselves without another person can lead to problems with insecurity, trust, enabling, clinginess, smothering, unhealthy attachment, addiction, and most of all, codependency. When two people are feeding off each other in a codependent relationship, that can cause real issues when the two people have to be apart for any reason and is a breeding ground for eventual negative feelings. Again, it feels good to be needed and it feels good to help our loved ones, but if you create a dependency, or an unhealthy attachment, it's eventually going to not balance out and one person in the relationship is going to need it more than the other. This imbalance of *need versus help* creates a dynamic of power and control which is unhealthy in any relationship.

I am not saying that we shouldn't help our loved ones. I believe we are put on this earth to do just that: to learn to love others and to help them along the way. I believe that is the entire purpose of life itself, quite actually, but there is a difference between helping someone and trying to save them. There is a difference between helping someone and enabling them. There's an old Chinese proverb that states, "Give a man a fish, and you feed him for a day. Teach a man to fish, and you feed him for a lifetime." We can give all the fish we have and feed others till we have no fish left, but if we allow others to *learn* how to fish, they will be self-sufficient and feed themselves for a lifetime. It's sometimes a fine line between helping and enabling, too. I am all for helping someone out of a tough situation or jam, helping someone when they need and want help. However, if someone repeatedly makes poor choices for themselves, gets themselves into the same or similar bad situations every time, without trying to help themselves, and/or expecting you to come and fix it for them, how are they ever going to learn how to help themselves or save themselves? This is when helping becomes enabling. Even if they don't ask or expect you to help them out of the mess that they've gotten themselves into and you continually "make everything okay again" for them, without them having to deal with the real consequences of their behavior, their actions, and their own choices, in the end, this is not helpful to them. In fact, it's quite damaging. Sometimes lessons must be learned the hard way for people to truly learn from their mistakes or the situations they have found themselves in. Tough love isn't the absence of love; it's loving a person from afar, letting them fall so they can learn to pick their own self up again.

I realize that It's great to feel needed. It's wonderful to know that you have *saved the day* for someone you rescued. It makes us feel important. But it's so crucial to not fall into that trap of needing that feeling of importance (and power), that feeling of knowing you are needed and that person couldn't have done it without *wonderful you* because that person needs to feel wonderful about themselves. They need to know that they can do it; they can help themselves, they can make better choices, and they need to know that when it comes down to it, they can count on themselves to survive. I know personally how very hard it is to watch someone you love self-destruct by making one terribly bad choice after another, or deliberately doing bad things to themselves, such as being addicted to drugs. Our nature when we see our loved ones hurting and suffering is to want to stop it, to do whatever we can to get that person out of their pain and suffering, because we love them. Unfortunately, some people need to hit their own rock bottom to understand and know which way is up. I won't lie and say this is easy to watch or easy to do, but if you truly love the person, you will let them live and learn. You can help them at times when it's appropriate, but you also must let them walk their path alone. You can't walk it for them. Besides, you have your own path to walk, and that's quite enough.

But some will say, "doesn't the Bible say to put others first and to love others before loving yourself?" Actually, no, it doesn't say that, nor is it recorded that Jesus Himself ever said that. What it does state is that we are to "love our neighbors *AS* ourselves."[7] It doesn't say *before* ourselves, or *more than* ourselves, but AS ourselves.

There are several different types of love. According to the Greeks, there's eros love, which involves sexual desire. Some would call this type of love lust. There's philia love, which is known as a love of the mind, or brotherly love, a sincere and platonic love. Some would call this type of love friendship. There's ludus love, which is a child-like, playful, fun kind of love. Some may refer to this type of love as infatuation. There's pragma love, which is referred to as a longstanding love, an everlasting love between a married couple which develops over a long period of time. Some people call this type of love commitment and involves understanding, compromise, and tolerance. Finally, there is what is referred to as the highest form of love, agape love, which is referred to as a love of the soul. It's called a selfless kind of love, a more spiritual love. It's the love you give without expecting anything in return. It is shown through charitable acts, compassion, sympathy, empathy, and is a universal type of love. People of the Christian religion also refer to agape love as God's love, and add that it's unconditional, meaning void of conditions placed on it or the person to receive such love[8]. And here's where I have a problem with that.

They say that God's love is unconditional. That God will love you regardless of any condition and requires nothing from you to give this love to you. I used to believe that comforting thought, until I was taught that I had to "invite Jesus into my heart," for Him to be there. So, that's what I did to receive God's unconditional love. Then they told me that wasn't enough. That I had to be baptized in the "Holy Spirit" and invite not only Jesus and God, but the Holy Spirit to come live in my heart, to be loved by God. It was a process they called being "born again." I had to be "born again" in order to receive God's love, to ensure my ticket into Heaven when I died. These all seemed like conditions to me. Furthermore, I learned that I had to repent of my sins, ask God for forgiveness, repeatedly, after every sin, which happened quite often, I will admit. There are some religious people who actually believe that if you die without first asking for forgiveness for your sins that you will actually be sent to Hell, not Heaven, by this unconditionally loving God. To some Catholics, babies who die without being baptized first never even have a chance. Nope, just straight to Hell. Sorry babies, you are shit out of luck. Then, they say God sometimes needs angel babies, but I guess not angel babies who weren't first baptized. And why would God need angel babies anyway? It's just something people say to comfort themselves and others when a baby or young child dies. They say that God needed another angel. But seriously, does He not have enough angels up there worshipping and praising him? Guess not. I was also told that even though God loves you unconditionally, he can simultaneously still send you to Hell. So, bottom line is that I do not think God's love is unconditional. (And I also kind of think He's a narcissist).

I am sure there are many other various kinds of love or names for the different kinds of love other than those I have mentioned here, but I think that oftentimes we confuse the emotion of love with other emotions, like obsession, addiction, attachment, even adoration and admiration. These, to me, are not love, but other emotions we think are love. It used to really bother me when I would hear someone say that, "It's not love if it doesn't make you crazy!" Bullshit. I even dare to disagree with the rock band, Def Leppard, too. Love DOESN'T HURT!

I also would hear people say that love is blind, I used to add that, it's also deaf and dumb! But, I have a different view on it now. Although I believe in the existence of the "honeymoon period" at the beginning of a romantic relationship, I do not think that true, actual love is blind. I think when someone loves someone else, they aren't blind. They see the other person's shortcomings or character defects, but they still love them, unconditionally. What I DO think is blind, though, and believe that people often confuse with love is obsession, addiction, and attachment to someone else. With these emotions, a person ends up either not seeing red flags in a relationship, doesn't see major problems/character defects in the other person (issues that the other person truly needs professional help with), and/or they will make excuses for unacceptable treatment/behavior towards them by the other person. This is not love. Love doesn't hurt. Obsession, addiction or attachment to another person can hurt, and hurt intensely.

This is just something I have learned through my own experience with having romantic feelings for another person and being in a relationship with them. I can truly say that Katie and I LOVE each other. We see each other's faults, but we love past them and we help each other to improve and overcome those shortcomings. I've been obsessed, addicted, and/or attached to people before and it really ended up hurting. But with loving Katie, our love never hurts and I am thankful for finally finding what is truly love. When you miss someone, you love, that hurts. It's the "missing" that hurts; it's your attachment to that person who is no longer there that hurts. Their absence hurts you and makes you feel sad. When you see someone, you love hurting, that hurts. Or when you see someone you love self-destructing, knowing you can't help them, that hurts. But the actual emotion of true love should not hurt. If it does, it's not love.

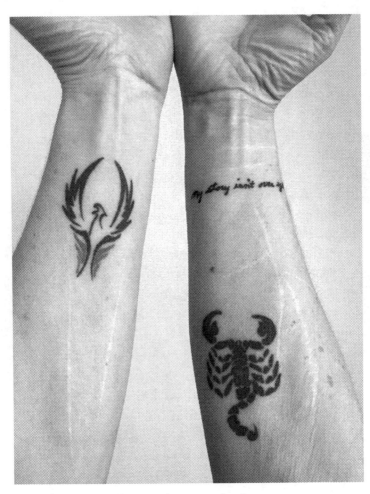

The Roadmap to the Scars

My drawing of my ECT experience

My loving partner, Katie and me

The day we adopted Rory

Mom and me

My Mom, me, and my Dad

Michael and me

My alter ego- Duke Ulysses Hunter

Melissa with her first published book,
Surviving Crazy: A Roadmap to the Scars

My SPIRITUAL JOURNEY

"A Quid Pro *No* Quo With God"

"A scientist will read dozens of books in his lifetime but still believes he has a lot more to learn. A religious person barely reads one book and believes he knows it all."[9]

To preface this essay, I want to say that all of what is written in here (in this entire book, in fact) is purely based on my opinion, views, and beliefs that I have developed thus far on my spiritual journey. There are reasons why I hold the beliefs concerning religion that I do. Many of the reasons are based on bad experiences that I have had throughout my entire life, regarding organized religion and the people who claimed to be Christians. I have found that many religious people are so bent on "keeping the Christ in Christmas" that they forget to keep the Christ in Christian. However, it is also based on enlightenment that I have experienced while trying to make sense of it all. I believe that more people have been hurt in the name of religion than just about any other thing and I wanted to know why that seemed to be the case. So, with an open mind, a fearless heart, and a dose of cold reality I began trying to answer all the questions that I just couldn't live with surrounding God. It was very frightening at first because I was always told NOT to question God. That He works in mysterious ways. I was told that we must trust that everything works out for the greater good, everything happens for a reason, which is God's reason, and it's all according to His master plan. He's the one in charge and who knows what is going on. He also knows what is going to happen in the future and I was expected to just trust and obey. Anything less than all of this would mean that I didn't have true faith. In my earlier years, I was terrified of being sent to the fiery pit of Hell to burn there forever while the Devil laughed and laughed at me for eternity. Then, the more I studied religion and listened to people preach religion, I discovered that there were more and more things about myself that definitely would ensure my ticket to eternal damnation. Many of these things about myself I felt that I was born with, was how God made me, and there were some beliefs that I just couldn't accept.

As a sheep, I struggled, because I wanted to think for myself. I didn't just want to blindly follow the masses or do what I was told to do, think what I was told to think, and feel what I was told to feel based on someone else's interpretation of a piece of literature written over 2,000 years ago. I didn't want to do things for the simple fact that "that's the way we've always done them," or because that's what my parent's parent's parent's parent's told them and then told me to believe. It just didn't seem genuine or right to me. So, I dared to commit the sin of questioning God and questioning the entire thing.

I know that this section of my book may upset a lot of people who believe differently than me, and that is never my intent, to upset people or hurt them. I honestly do get why some people need to believe what they believe. Who am I to tell someone who has just lost a dear loved one that the red cardinal in their yard is not their loved one assuring them that he or she is okay, or at peace, or is watching over them as they grieve their loss? I get that things like this comfort people, make them feel better, gives them peace, and is something to hold on to, to believe in. So, I am not saying that things like this are definitely not true, because honestly, I don't know for sure that it is a fact that such beliefs aren't true. I also do not have any scientific proof that things like this ARE true, but that's irrelevant.

The only real fact one will read in this book is the that when dealing with spiritual matters, like religious faith and views on God, opinions are all anyone's beliefs and views really are. I realize even just saying this will piss some people off. They will say that their religious beliefs are not just opinions, but facts, damn it! However, since faith cannot be proven and no empirical evidence can be given on these things, no one really can know for sure, based on the other facts that are known (and proven) about this topic. These things I write about are things I believe, think, and feel. I am not insisting that they become your beliefs, thoughts, and feelings. I am not even defending a position here, concerning what I now believe about God and religion. So, as you read this, please do not let your faith be shaken, don't let it take away any comfort you may be receiving from your beliefs. Just take it as it is, which is just my own opinion. Naturally, I encourage thinking for yourself as you continue your own journey to finding yourself, but the bottom line is that your journey is your journey, and this book is my journey. Neither have to be right or wrong. It is only important to continue on.

With that being said, if God did create me, I believe He/She made me left-handed, brown haired, with bipolar disorder, gay, with a sense of humor, and all my other innate attributes with which I believe I was born. God also gave me a curious and inquisitive mind. I do not believe that it is a sin to be curious, no matter what "they" say curiosity did to the cat. Nor do I believe it is a sin to question things, even when dealing with authority, even with what some consider to be the highest authority, God. I do, on the other hand, think that it *is* necessary TO question things, especially authority. If we never questioned things, we would still believe that the earth is flat, that you can cure someone's ailments by attaching leeches to his body, or that those who are sick have a demon inside them that needs to be cast out. Wait a minute. Some of us still believe in those examples, even the last one. Consider why most people say, "God bless you," when you sneeze. Luckily for the sick, most doctors do not still believe in the healing power of leeches or in the power of Christ to compel you. Why? It is because they questioned things.

The reason I believe that it is most important to question the "men in charge," or authority in general, is because we have seen so many times in our history where those who claimed to have the answers were simply wrong. There are doctors who give misdiagnoses and when this happens, sometimes people die. We all make mistakes and oversights, but when an authority figure makes a mistake, many often suffer the consequences of that mistake. Who was in charge of picking that sign language interpreter who stood next to former president Obama when he was in Africa at Nelson Mandela's funeral? Remember that? How did that interpreter's serious and potentially violent mental illness go unnoticed? That incident could have turned out tragic because of that oversight. Our former United States president could have been injured or even killed had the interpreter's schizophrenia been worse at that time. No violence occurred in that incident, thankfully, and the story faded from the news to a *Saturday Night Live* skit, at which we were all expected to laugh and find humor in. If someone would have questioned the choosing of that interpreter, even though he had been an interpreter in Africa for a long time and had assisted in many speeches, he may have been able to get better help for his mental illness. At the very least, he would not have late night comedy television people joking about how absurd he looked when his schizophrenia made him lose his concentration and started making hand symbols that hearing impaired viewers knew was not, in fact, official sign language.

If the Surgeon General would announce today that she was wrong in their finding and that cigarettes cause cancer, how many people would be ripping off their nicotine patches as she spoke and resume smoking. How many times have we heard on the evening news that something, say frozen peas, are extremely good for you and can ward off disease, so we go out and fill our freezers with peas, only to watch the evening news the next night and hear that "studies have proven that peas are not in fact good for us, instead they cause liver damage." Now, I am exaggerating here to illustrate a point.

Questioning is a normal, natural, and positive thing to do. Questioning authority, or *those in charge,* is an absolutely necessary thing to do, in my opinion. Questioning those who have authority over other people and their civil rights is ultimately important. I personally have questioned and majorly disagreed with the politicians in Washington who allowed a set group of people's religious beliefs dictate my right to marry who I love, as a gay person. Is it just to deny someone's human rights based on someone else's faith? I do not believe it is just or right, nor do the millions of other gay people who are demanding to simply have the same rights as everyone else. Not more rights, not better rights, but the same rights. If it *feels* "wrong," we believe it *is* wrong, without questioning it. We do not need to feel guilt for questioning things, either, like some religions profess. Should we have felt guilt when we questioned Adolf Hitler's authority in Nazi Germany? It is a good and often life-saving notion to question things. So, why shouldn't we question the ultimate authority figure for some, God, who many believe expects us to obey His commands and laws? Why do some people say that we shouldn't question those things?

I have seen several bumper stickers on automobiles throughout my life that stated: QUESTION AUTHORITY, but the day I saw the first bumper sticker that instructed me to QUESTION REALITY, I knew people were further along on the right track. To this day, however, I have never seen a bumper sticker that read: QUESTION GOD. Why? Maybe there are bumper stickers out there and I just haven't seen any, but why aren't those bumper stickers as common as the stickers that read QUESTION AUTHORITY? Maybe the reason is because we, as a people or particular society, have not progressed that far yet. I don't think I would have ever seen an automobile proudly bearing a bumper sticker that read QUESTION AUTHORITY back in the 1950's. So, maybe we just aren't there yet, in 2017. OR maybe the reason why our cars don't bear that bumper sticker that tells us to QUESTION GOD is because a lot us are afraid we will be struck by God's holy rod of lightning and killed if we dare? Let me just add here that thinking about and deciding where you stand spiritually is an essential part of your journey of finding yourself. Questioning God and His motives are part of it because ultimately questioning God is questioning yourself.

"IT IS BETTER TO BE FEARED THAN LOVED, IF YOU CANNOT BE BOTH."[10]

-Niccolo Machiavelli (and God?)

Fear is as powerful a motivator to do things as it is a motivator for us not to do things. How many of us obey laws because we are afraid of the consequences we may receive if we don't? This brings me to the topic of altruism and back to unconditional love. Altruism is the selfless concern for the wellbeing of others. Is there such a thing as true altruism? I mean complete, selfless, unconditional love and concern often shown through altruistic acts of kindness towards others. I personally don't think so. At best, it's extremely rare to find in others. Some of us call acts of kindness towards others "good deeds." It's my experience that this term for kindness is usually used by Christians and other religious folks. The reason why I don't believe in complete, pure, unconditional love for others shown through these good deeds is that there is usually a motivating factor involved behind them. Why do people do them? On the surface one might think it's because that person believes it's the "right" thing to do, but why? I believe that certain people's underlying motivation, even subconsciously, is because of two factors: fear and reward. Many people fear what will happen to their souls when they die. They fear God's punishment of burning forever and ever in the fiery pit of

Hell. Deep down, I believe that this is why some people do those good deeds. They fear what would happen if they weren't seen as good people, doing good deeds for others, and they fear punishment. Remember, most of us don't just obey the speed limit signs because it's the law or the "right thing to do." Most of us obey laws because we fear the consequences if we don't obey. We fear punishment and repercussion. It's really not that different with God's laws.

Thinking back to that small religious cult that I was a part of when I was a teen, I remember how the two gurus (leaders) would describe these gems and jewels we would get in our Heavenly crown for each and every good deed that we did. It was supposed to be a selling factor to get us to want to do more good deeds, so we would get more jewels in our crown, but it didn't work that way for me. I just kept thinking how hats flatten my hair. A heavy crown would make my hair look uglier and that with each jewel I would earn in my crown, it was only going to make that thing heavier. Upon deeper thought, though, it made me question the validity of a good deed. Was it really a selfless act of kindness if we were doing it to get something in return, even if we didn't get the reward until we died and entered Heaven?

An unconditional act of kindness has no conditions! That's why it's called unconditional! I knew then that if I did something good for someone expecting something in return, that it was not actually a selfless act of kindness or goodwill towards men. If you don't believe you do things for people in order to get something in return, think about the times you hold the door for someone and they stroll right in past you without saying thank you or even acknowledging that you just did some great act of kindness for them by holding the door. Most of us at least expect a thank you from the person we do anything for, anything such as loaning money, offering other assistance, giving a gift to someone, or yes, even holding the door. Expecting anything in return is a condition you place on your kindness and good deeds. This is why I don't believe that true altruism exists in most people. We give to get. It's not obvious, and what you get in return for giving might even be a byproduct that you want and aren't even aware that you are wanting.

Since most of us like to feel appreciated, especially when we do something nice or when we are being "good" (a good person), that makes true altruism null and void. We don't like to think about our kindness towards others in this way. We want to think we are being good just for the sake of being good, not because we fear Hell or want to get to Heaven, or even want an acknowledgement such as a simple thank you. Sometimes people will do nice things for other people because it makes them feel good. Feeling good is a reward, though, is it not? But the need to feel good, the need to be appreciated, and the need to be acknowledged are all human emotions, so don't beat yourself up too badly. Just be aware of your deeper, hidden motives when you are doing that altruistic, selfless, unconditional act of kindness. Most people's highest power, God, motivates His followers through reward and punishment, too. So, it's really something we have learned or have been conditioned by religion. And now it's time for me to quote one of my favorite random quotes that you may or may not connect to this topic:

"Religion is for people who are afraid of going to Hell. Spirituality is for people who have already been there." -Vine Deloria Jr. (and many others)

Many of us even follow society's norms, which aren't even laws, because we are afraid to stand out in society, or to some worse yet, not belong. Often fear keeps us oppressed. Some gay people all over the world stay in the proverbial closet all their lives because they fear persecution. They suppress who they really are and deny themselves happiness because of fear. I read a saying that stated there are 365 verses or times "fear not" is mentioned in the Bible. It's a comforting thought to some, that God tells us 365 times, coincidentally once for every day in the year, that we should fear not…. the things in this world, but to put our trust in Him. However, upon researching this statistic further, I found that this is just a cutesy saying for believers. It actually does not state "fear not" 365 times. In fact, many people who have researched this could not even find 100 times where it states in the Bible, "fear not." Regardless of this actual number, believers are supposed to feel safe or comfortable from knowing that their God tells them to not fear so much and that He will protect them. I read a more accurate study that stated that the word *fear* itself can be found over 400 times in the Bible, in 384 verses. In even further reading of this study, it explained that fear of God was vital for salvation. The writer of the study went on to state that those who do not fear God will not be saved from the fiery pit of Hell that the Bible tells us we will be thrown into where we will burn forever for not living a godly life of obeying God's commandments. That, to me, is some fearful shit.

So, we see here that in this scenario, acceptance of God, belief in God, and fearing God are all vital in order to be "saved." Both instructions use the word fear. God tells us **not** to fear this world and God tells us **to** fear Him, according to what is written in the Bible. I read this as God wanting us to be afraid of Him, including being afraid of His punishments if we do not fear Him. This is not as comforting of a thought when talking about fear. Religious people have tried to explain to me that when the Bible instructs us *to fear* God, the word fear does not have the same meaning as it does when instructing us to *NOT* fear things of this world. Suddenly, the word fear means to have reverence for or respect when dealing with "fearing God." We aren't supposed to read scriptures stating to FEAR GOD as meaning that we need to be afraid of Him. Instead, we are supposed to RESPECT and have reverence for Him. But, what if God really meant it the other way around? Maybe we are supposed to be AFRAID of God and His punishments, but to have RESPECT (not fear) for the things of this world? This does not make sense to most Christians, therefore, they do not believe that is the case, that it's the other way around about fear and respect. I personally think that the Bible maybe meant both definitions of fear when talking about God. We are to honor and respect Him, but we should be afraid of Him. What would the reason be for insisting upon the belief that if a person does not believe in God, there will be a consequence of getting damned to a horrible, painful, burning, everlasting inferno called Hell?

So, fear is one reason we do not question things. If the

Bible states or even simply implies that God does not want us to question Him and this is one of His commandments, and disobeying His commandments will land us in Hell, who would be brave enough to question Him? Another reason people don't question things is because they just don't want to know the answer. If most people were given a book about their entire life, they would not read the ending of it to find out how they die because they would rather not know that answer, in my opinion. Some people just have a less inquisitive mind, perhaps, so they don't feel the need or the desire to question things. After all, questioning things takes work. It takes brain work that some people can't afford. It takes thinking for yourself, instead of being a sheep who follows. And some people do things without questioning them because "that's the way we've always done it." Do most people question why they put a decorated dying pine tree in their living room every year at Christmas time? No. Most of them just do it. There are countless other mindless traditions people continue without ever wondering why or researching how the tradition even began.

Maybe we should consider that some people are just lazy thinkers who want others to do their thinking for them. I mean, it takes less mind work to just do what others say or what others have always done, or to just do what you are told to do, right? It takes less mental effort to just do what others say and not question it, especially if those others are our parents, God, or other authority figures. If a child asks her parents why they must do something that the parent tells them to do, oftentimes the parent's answer is "because I said so!" I believe this is the basis for the belief in a book that was written by the hands of men (and a few women) over two thousand years ago, during a different time and era, but supposed to be taken as the gospel word right out of God's mouth for all of us to follow today. Who first told you that you were supposed to believe in the Bible?

As I was growing up, my parents were not religious in that they did not attend church every Sunday or expect me to attend. Nor was I surrounded by a ton of extremely religious people as a small child, but somehow it was implied that I was supposed to believe in God and to just assume that the Bible was the truth. My parent's parents might have told or implied to them that this was common, factual knowledge as well. And so on. No one ever sat me down and said, "this is WHY we believe that the Bible is God's word," other than "because it says so." My family, or anyone else I was with, certainly did not encourage me to question it. So, I grew up with the belief that the Bible was not a work of fictional literature, but that everything in it was completely true. I was just supposed to believe it and that was my faith. That's at least how my faith started.

Now that we have discussed possible reasons for people not to want to question things, let's look at some of the reasons why they do. When people do question things, it is for a variety of reasons. Some of those include: simple curiosity, trust issues, skepticism (doubt) and the need to know. But I believe the most common reason why people question things is because something doesn't make sense. The thing(s) in question doesn't serve the questioner. They don't understand it and it doesn't work for them, meaning they question the validity of it because there are other options (answers) to consider. Religion and religious faith/beliefs are among the most common things that I believe people question nowadays. However, this particular questioning, for some people, holds the most guilt. In many religions, we are told NOT to question. After all, the basis of religious faith is "believing without seeing," without fact or proof. Therefore, many believe that if we do question our faith, then we do not really *have* faith. There's a well-known statement that "God works in mysterious ways and we are not to question God." But, wasn't it our Creator who gave us the very nature to love a good mystery and want to read that book to the end to find out the answer to the mystery? Many movie goers become very upset if a movie ends without a real ending, even if that ending is tragic. We want to know. Now, a lot of us want a movie or book to question and have an answer/solution to that question. The plot to most stories involves some type of problem that needs to be worked out or fixed, and unfortunately, some demand a happily ever after. I do not believe the Bible has a definite ending where it answers every contradiction in it and answers the ultimate mystery, but many would disagree. "That's where faith comes in," I am told. "That's where you just have to believe everything in it because it is the Word of God breathed into the men (and those couple of women) who wrote it. We just must trust the ending, "He will return for us some day." God will save the day. "Jesus saves." But how does Jesus save?

If you break it down, consider all of it, who do you think is actually going to make it into God's Heaven? Some people will answer that those who believed in Him, invited Him into their heart will make it into Heaven. Others will add that to get that holy ticket into the gates, people must also have gotten baptized in the Holy Spirit. And not only baptized in the Spirit but also sent the Holy Spirit a special invitation to join Jesus in the domain of your hollow muscular organ that lies slightly to the left of the midline of your chest, which suddenly makes you become "born again." While others will slightly disagree, and say that those who make the cut into Heaven will be those who followed the commandments and asked for forgiveness immediately after each sin. Or will it be those who spread the word about God and how to be saved from Hell and did good deeds? How about those who have enough jewels in their heavenly crown, and those who believed without question? Maybe it requires all of the above, but most importantly, just don't question it. And I am not okay with that, so I question it. I dared to question God. I wanted a simple, direct quid pro quo with Him, but I always ended up getting a "quid pro **no** quo." So finally, I decided that the only way *Jesus saves* is by switching His car insurance to *Geico*.

"If I didn't have a sense of humor, I'd have no sense at all." - Melissa Ross

MAYBE THE BIBLE ISN'T THE "GOSPEL?"

As I grew into adulthood, I didn't immediately announce that I had countless unanswered questions about God and the Bible, because of fear. I remember being excited to take an unorthodox college class called The Bible as Literature, because I was eager to learn more about it since I wasn't satisfied by a preacher telling me his interpretations of the Bible through church service. Preachers rarely state in church as they are ministering that what they are telling the churchgoers is merely their opinion of what he or she has read in the Bible. They don't say that their sermons are their beliefs on what the Bible says based on their interpretations of it. Instead, they preach the Word of God as complete truth, insisting that there is only one correct interpretation of each scripture they are reading. This was not the case in my Bible as Literature class. I remember several of the students on that first day of class becoming quite unpleasantly surprised that in this course, the Bible was going to be studied as a fictional piece of literature and not God's Word. In fact, that first day the professor explained this, a few students actually stood up and walked out of the classroom immediately.

Honestly, I even felt a tinge of guilt for even thinking about the possibility of not believing that everything in the Bible really happened, but I stayed in that class and I am glad I did. I learned to look at the Bible more objectively and that course made me able to make more sense out of it. One of the many things in the Bible that I couldn't wrap my head around was how Jonah survived in the belly of that whale all that time and came out of the whale's mouth alive, as written in the scriptures. It made much more sense to me that stories in the Bible like that were written as parables to illustrate a point, but did not actually and literally happen. There's a scripture in the book of Proverbs that reads, "Whoever spares the rod hates their children, but the one who loves their children is careful to discipline them."[11] I was relieved to learn in the class that *spare the rod, spoil the child* does not mean that God wants parents to beat their children into submission for the children to grow up and be honest, responsible adults. Sadly, however, some parents do quote and use that particular scripture to justify physically abusing their children to this very day.

I ended up really enjoying that class because it made me feel less afraid to admit that I had questions surrounding God, and the Bible in general. I also learned that the Bible wasn't the only book written about the nature of God and it was not the end all, be all word that I originally was expected to believe. There were these books called "missing scrolls of the Bible" that had been found throughout the years in addition to the Bible. Whether these missing scriptures truly got lost or were purposely left out of the Bible for assorted reasons and motives by the authors of the Bible is also debatable. Some facts become inconvenient truths, and when an author is trying to portray a particular set of values or beliefs, these facts are often omitted. If a group of men had an agenda of keeping only men in power and wanted to further oppress women, then they might likely *keep* the verses in the Bible that state that women should not speak up in church, but should be obedient to men, for instance.

These men would also minimize the importance of women during biblical days, discounting their true value and worth, but offering up only a couple of books in the Bible actually written about women, by women. I could see why the male authors of the Bible would definitely want to leave out things about Adam, the first man in the beginning of creation, like Adam having a wife before Eve, whose name was Lilith. I think Lilith was excluded from the Bible because she would not bow down to Adam and insisted on being his equal. A person doesn't have to believe that that missing story from the Bible is true to recognize that men are clearly represented as superior to women in the scriptures that did not go "missing" from, or purposely excluded from, the Bible, even if it was a *woman* who gave birth to God (Jesus). Is it just a coincidence that men wrote and/or decided what was relevant to keep in the Bible?

We are told that our God is our Heavenly Father, a male, that has created us with no help from a female God, and we are all His children. Do you think that if it were mostly women who wrote the Bible, it would be explained to us that God is our Heavenly Mother, a female Creator, who bore us into existence onto this great planet? We call our planet "Mother Earth" because she gives birth to nature and in a sense, is a creator of life. Just as with a male and his sperm, without a female's egg, the miracle of life on this earth does not happen. So why are we expected to believe that only a single male God created the first life, universe and everything in it?

The male version of the Bible that we are expected

to believe as God's truth has directly influenced how our society was formed and how it struggles to progress. It was only in my grandmother's lifetime that women were given the right to vote (1920). Before that, women had no say in who was chosen to be in charge of things. To this day, there are jobs all over the country where men and women do the exact same thing, but women get paid less than men. As a woman, knowing these things makes me question the validity of the Bible even more so.

Imagine a scenario where a father and young child are talking. The child says to the father, "I really love you with all my heart, Father. I believe in what you teach me and try to follow your rules." The father in return says, "Well, I don't believe that you truly do love me. So, I am going to put you to a test." Then, the father allows the child's mother to be killed. The child says, "I still love you, Father." So, then the father allows someone to repeatedly burn the child with cigarettes all over his little body. The child whispers in pain, "I still love you, Father." Finally, the father just nearly beats his child to death to see if the child will still love him. Some would call this outrageous abuse. Others choose to call it faith. Sounds absurd, right? Why would a father who sincerely loves his child, need to test the child's love for him like that? I stated that others would choose to call this a test of faith because an even worse scenario happened to a devote follower of God named Job. In the Bible, the book of Job describes this in detail. In it, God wants to see if Job really does love Him, so he causes or allows all these terrible afflictions to happen to Job to see if he will remain steadfast in his faith. If any parent would do that to their child in this life, I believe it would be called severe child abuse and not looked upon as favorable. This story of Job is in the Bible, so it is to be taken as completely true. That's the thing about the Bible, in my opinion; no one gets to decide which stories are just fables, parables, or illustrations to prove a point, versus what is to be taken literally, as something that absolutely happened the exact way it was described.

This is the problem I have with what some refer to as "cafeteria Christians." A cafeteria Christian picks and chooses what he or she wants to take as literal in the Bible, decides what truths or laws are still relevant to this day and age, and which ones we should simply see as outdated or no longer practiced. For example, we no longer sell our daughters into marriage for three goats and a lamb, as once practiced in the Bible. But some people insist that the couple times in the Bible where it refers to homosexuality as being a sin is still quite actual and should be seen as a law today. The one scripture referring to this that most like to quote from is from the book of Leviticus. It's a section regarding hygiene and cleanliness as being part of the law and it lists such sins as men shaving their beards, the sin of eating shellfish (such as shrimp), or eating a dirty, filthy pig (pork). In amongst these lines is where you will find the famous *man should not lie with another man* scripture and then it goes on further to state that men should not have sex with women while the woman is on her menstrual cycle[12]. It is my opinion and belief that the "man should not lie with another man..." verse in the grouping has more to do about cleanliness and diseases at that time, rather than homosexuality, itself, being a sin. And since nowadays some men want to shave their beards, and people enjoy the taste of things like shrimp and pork, we are told that those particular scriptures are outdated. Since we have learned new things like ways to clean food properly, so we don't get sick from eating those certain foods, we are told to disregard those scriptures surrounding such, for they are no longer applicable. Men still can get diseases from having sex with other men, but now we are more educated about preventing that from happening by using things like condoms, which they obviously didn't have back in biblical days. I just don't believe that God would intend to have a morality code thrown in a discussion about cleanliness.

And that particular Old Testament scripture from Leviticus, that people like to quote to try and prove that God says being gay is a sin didn't even make it into one of the top ten commandments. To my knowledge, Jesus makes no mention against homosexuality in the New Testament. Yet, since many of us (I'll say it, mostly men) still fear, are threatened by, and hate what we don't understand or what we don't agree with, we are supposed to uphold the scripture in the middle of all that discussion and believe that being gay is a sin. That "God hates fags." Are you serious? I think it's quite convenient, ironic and completely absurd to believe that God would hate a person simply because of loving someone of the same sex.

As mentioned, most of those few scriptures that do relate to homosexuality are found in the Old Testament, the first books of the Bible where God is an angry, vengeful, unforgiving God. The second part of the Bible is called the New Testament because it was to be seen as the new law, where God gave us His only son to die for us, to forgive us of sins, and once Jesus was on the scene, God was seen as a much more loving, compassionate God. A clear example of the difference between the Old and New Testament is from an actual New Testament scripture that Jesus supposedly actually said to the people, "You have heard it said, an eye for an eye, a tooth for a tooth. But, I tell you, do not resist an evil person. If anyone slaps you on the right cheek, turn to him the other cheek also. If anyone wants to sue you and take your shirt, hand over your coat, as well. If anyone forces you to go one mile, go with them two miles..." This scripture, which is found in Matthew 5:38-48[13] of the Holy Bible, then goes on with Jesus instructing us to "love our enemies and do good to those who hurt us." This example should illustrate how the Bible went from an angry, bitter, vengeful God from the Old Testament who tells us to gouge out someone's eye who has gouged out ours first, to a much more loving, compassionate, kind God of Jesus Christ who tells us to turn the other cheek. In my opinion, when Jesus was brought into the world to save it from sin and to teach us how to love in the New Testament, then the Old Testament was no longer the law of the land, yet people still love to quote from the Old Testament, out of context no less, to support their own beliefs.

Unfortunately, this becomes a very big problem for some when these people not only use it to support their personal beliefs, but to create laws that all others must obey based on those particular people's personal religious beliefs. I have said it many times, when our constitution and America itself stands for freedom of religion, it should also include freedom *from* religion. This is partly why the separation of church and state is so very important. Somehow this country went from being founded based on people fleeing from religious persecution to religious people persecuting others who do not share the same beliefs and creating laws to enforce a particular religion's beliefs onto someone else, making it a punishable crime if they do not believe and follow the same beliefs. An example of this would be the just recently rescinded law that prohibited others who love people of their same sex to marry one another because of religious beliefs. To this day, however, in this great country of the United States of America, people who are LGBT do not have all of the same equal rights as heterosexuals do. A person can still be fired from his/her job, simply for being gay, lesbian, bisexual or transgender. And there are many religious people who call themselves Christians and still believe that being who you are, being how God created you (being LGBT), is undeniably a sin against God.

Another reason why the separation of church and state is so important is because there are so many different religions, so many different Gods to believe in and none of them are right or wrong. When I hear religious people insisting on prayer in school, I would bet money that they don't mean letting each child have a prayer mat so he or she can pray to Allah. In America, we must respect all people's beliefs, not just Christian beliefs, but even the complete non-believers (atheists) as well, for this country truly to be the land of freedom. I personally do not think that "one nation, under God" should be included in the pledge of allegiance, either, because not all Americans believe in God. It still baffles my mind as to why we must put our hand on the Bible during a state proceeding, when we are told to swear to tell the truth. Do you think an atheist putting his hand on a book that he doesn't see as anything but a piece of literature is going to compel him or her to swear to tell the truth? In my mind, that's ridiculous. But, that is the way we've always done it and people like routine/ritual, especially if it represents their own beliefs.

Some people will cling to old beliefs like their lives depended on it. They will not even consider any other way of thinking or doing because, like I said before, they will say it's the way they've always done it. It's what they've always believed. It's what they were taught to believe and it would be wrong or a sin to believe anything different, even if it is proven by fact and science to be untrue. If you don't believe this, ask yourself why we still celebrate Columbus Day, when we have come to find that Christopher Columbus was not actually the one to discover America. We didn't change the holiday to Leif Erikson Day when we thought we had uncovered the fact that a Viking was really the first to discover America. Do you know what was actually discovered, though? They discovered that the Native American Indians/Indigenous people were here first. That leads me to the holiday that I refer to not as Thanksgiving Day, but "Slaughtering the Native Americans Day," which is, in a sense, what happened. People only want to think of the pilgrims who they believe founded Plymouth Rock as eating a big, peaceful meal with the Native Americans who offered us corn and other goods. We ignore the part of history where the Europeans brought smallpox with them, which killed many of the Native American Indians. Why? I think it's because that fact is ugly and we don't like ugly. We don't want to appear as an ugly and/or cruel people, so we stick with celebrating Columbus Day and give thanks on Thanksgiving Day. I think many people would be shocked if they researched the origins of most of the religious and even non-religious holidays that we still celebrate. Nobody wants to question Thanksgiving and ruin the opportunity for us to overstuff our faces with a delicious meal that we already must tolerate "difficult to deal with" relatives in order to get to eat. Don't fuck with the turkey!

So, people's beliefs still really motivate them to behave in certain ways and refrain from behaving in other ways. This brings me to one of my biggest confusions of them all when dealing with religion. Why does God let bad things happen to good people? Why does God let bad things happen at all, but especially to His most devoted, faithful followers? At this point, I would like to insert a few lines from one of my favorite movies, *Silence of the Lambs*.

"I collect church collapses, recreationally. Did you see the recent one in Sicily? Marvelous! The facade fell on sixty-five grandmothers at a special mass. Was that evil? If so, who did it? If He's up there, He just loves it, Officer Starling. Typhoid and swans- it all comes from the same place."[14]

-Hannibal Lecter

There are several books written in attempts to answer why bad things happen to good people. There's actually a book with that exact title. But since you are reading this book right now, I will tell you one way it has been explained to me. It rains on the good and the bad. That one, I will buy, but the other excuses for the horrible things that happen to truly, sincerely decent people, I just won't accept. I don't believe that God needs more angels and that's why my grandmother suffered with cancer for five long years and died a horrible death. I have asked why God didn't answer my prayer, so many people's prayers because she was on so many "prayer chains" at different churches. Why didn't God heal my grandmother? Why did he let her die of lung cancer? The most real and honest answer I have ever been given was by the preacher who performed my grandmother's funeral service that day back in 1994. He told me that she died of lung cancer because she smoked cigarettes all her life. I remember being furious at the time, shouting to God up in the evening sky, "FUCK YOU," when I was 23 years old and a preacher was telling me this truth. I wanted him to tell me why God did not heal my grandmother or why God didn't hear our prayers. The preacher never explained this part to me, he simply told me the facts, and at that time in my life, I certainly was not ready to hear or acknowledge facts, especially regarding God and religion, and my gram dying of cancer. I expected that preacher to give me some bullshit that I could really take to heart, something like "God needed another angel," or "God works in mysterious ways and we aren't to question God." He could have even said that saying "everything happens for a reason…and for the greater good, according to God's plan." As if something would ever be good enough of a reason to justify God allowing my grandmother to suffer and die like that. But that particular preacher didn't give me any bullshit faith or hope to hold on to, to comfort me in my time of grief and need. Nope. And I hated him for a long, long time after that, in part because of his explanation that it was my grandmother's fault that she died. I know now that he wasn't blaming her or saying it was truly her fault, just that smoking causes cancer and will kill you. But, MOST preachers and religious gurus WILL try to offer up a loving explanation as to why God allows suffering. I just didn't ask the right preacher at that time.

Back then, I questioned the scripture from the Bible that stated, *Ask and ye shall receive*,[15] because I thought that it meant that all you had to do was ask God for what you wanted/needed and you would receive it from Him. That's what the people from the church assured me as well, so I counted on that when I prayed so hard for God to heal my gram. I learned later that the rest of that scripture that is not included in the Bible ends not with a solution, but an answer. The answer from God concerning your request can sometimes be NO. Ask and ye shall receive…an answer, but it may not be the answer that you so desire and need. That explanation made more sense. God isn't always going to answer your prayers with a yes, or a give a solution that you want or even need. Sometimes the answer isn't even yes or no, but "wait." So, it made me wonder how God determined which prayers He would answer with a yes verses a no or a wait. How did He decide that? Did He base His decision on how long a person was on their knees praying? Was it based on the amount of prayers He received that day? Was it based on God's belief of the importance of the prayer? Was it based on how good of a person the one praying was or how often he/she goes to church, preaching the word, tithes, WHAT? What was it that made God decide who to heal and who to let suffer and die a painful death? Was it truly based on the "greater good" or God's will or His master plan?

I personally cannot think of ANY reason God would have that would be good enough to justify a little child being raped, tortured, and killed by his own parent's hand, or any hand for that matter. God can't need baby angels that badly. When I think of all the severe suffering in the world, it does make me question things, like God. Finding yourself also includes finding where you stand spiritually, and I have basically decided that I would rather believe that there's no God rather than believe in a God who would allow such suffering. I know that technically makes me an atheist. However, I don't consider myself an atheist because I truly do not know if God exists. I can't prove or disprove His existence, so I guess that makes me an agnostic. People tell me "God loves you!" and to that I reply "Yeah, and so does Santa Claus."[16] (Which is a line from a movie, *The Most Hated Woman in America*, a movie about Madalyn Murray O'Hair: an atheist activist whose efforts led to the Supreme Court ruling banning official Bible readings in public schools).

It makes me further wonder that if bad things happen to us all, even the people who are trying their very best to obey God and His Good Book, why do people continue to try to be "good" when they know that bad stuff will still continue to happen to them on occasion? Why do they still pray for things, when we've been told that either God doesn't intercede or that God is going to do pretty much what God wants to do, because it's all been planned. It's all a part of God's master plan. And if God knows what is going to happen already in the future, then how do you explain free will? How are we free to choose to sin or not to sin, and how can our will truly be considered free if it's preordained, and our lives are predestined, already planned? I have come to the conclusion that fear is still the highest motivating factor as to why many people continue to do good deeds even when bad things continuously happen to them. It's why the Christian chicken crossed the road….to get to the other side.

WWJD?

So, I'm leaving for work one morning, already late because I was engrossed in watching Fox News, when I realized I had no pop for work and had to stop at Wal-Mart. I grab my pop, go through the checkout line behind this woman with two kids using food stamps. I always feel the strong need to inspect everything people who use food stamps buy with my tax money. Sure enough, she had a bag of potato chips in one of her many bags! Anyway, as I am ready to cross the parking lot to get to my car, the same woman holding a crying kid in each arm, trying to push a cart full of groceries, asks for my help. She says, "Can you help me push my cart to my car?" I knew that the later I was going to get into work, the more my pay was going to be docked, so I hesitated for a moment. She has two arms and two legs, just like me, and I didn't force her to have kids that she couldn't handle grocery shopping with. I mean, she didn't PHYSICALLY look disabled or anything. But, I thought, "WWJD (What Would Jesus Do?)" So, I said, "Sure, I will help you, but first let me give you this drug test to make sure you aren't on drugs." (Because I ain"t helping some drug addict!) I pulled the little drug kit out that I always carry with me and gave her the test. Luckily for her, she passed. So, I agreed to push her cart to her car while she struggled with carrying her two unruly children. As she is trying to get the one kid in the car seat, it started to rain. She tried to hurry and says, "I wish I had an umbrella." I looked at her and thought to myself, "If you would have just had one kid instead of two that you don't seem to be able to handle, then you probably could afford to buy an umbrella." But, I didn't say that out loud to her, of course, because I'm a Christian. So, she gets her kids settled in and empties the shopping cart. I was already late for work and didn't want to take the time to return the cart back to the store, so I just pushed the cart out of the way, thinking, "I hope God sees this kind act that I am doing, and this bitch better say thank you," which she does, and so I head to my car. I look back at her and the woman suddenly turns into an angel. I immediately think "OMG! Oh my God, this was a test! God was testing me!" So, I smiled at the angel and said, "I did what Jesus would have done, right?" And the angel replies, "No. Jesus would have returned the cart."

(AND THAT, MY FRIENDS, IS CALLED SARCASM. My mom wanted me to make sure the reader knew that I just made this whole story up to illustrate a point. The story is fiction).

GOD'S COMPLEX
(a poem by Melissa Ross)

I've got an idea. Let Us throw some rocks in the air,
We'll make one rock "earth" and the rest I don't care.

I'll pollute it with people, similar to You and Me,
It's getting kind of boring, just talking with Us Three.

For I am feeling a bit lonely and I'm needing to be loved,
We'll watch over these people, of course, from Up Above.

They'll be Our entertainment, and We'll
give them a choice to be saved,
I'll create a damnation of Hell, for
those who won't behave.

I'll let them believe they have free will,
and not force them to follow Me,
But, if they don't fear and respect, then
they'll go into the Fiery Sea.

Which one in their right mind will not
choose Me to love and obey?
I'll tell them if they do love Me, then
I will make everything okay.

Oh the questions they will have when
I don't follow through,
I'll then just tell them not to question
and that patience is a virtue.

After I did all of this, there were still
those who refused to trust,
I must be feared and respected! I must be loved, I must!

For Us Three are Me, can't you see,
and that's not enough anymore,
We're "Father, Son, and Holy Ghost"
but no one to fight over Me for.

So, one of Us needs to go down there
and show them Love's meaning,
You picked the shortest straw, Jesus, so
You'll be leaving by this evening.

This need to be loved and worshipped is
what began this whole rat race,
If He could have just learned to love Himself,
none of us would be in this place.

A MOMENT OF HUMANITY (True story)

A wolf in "sheeple's" clothing came to my door one day attempting to share his "good news" with me. He generously told me of his faith and insisted mine was wrong. He stood in my doorway, arguing with me about things that he did not have proof of and were not facts. He warned me of my sinful nature and the perils of it, if I did not change my wicked ways. I am, of course, referring to the Christian couple that came to my door, shoving a Bible track in my face, telling me that God loves the sinner, but hates the sin, after I informed him that I was gay. (He came to MY door, but they say that gay people are the ones with the agenda?) I told him that I was happy in my own faith and that I believed God made me that way (gay). "It is not a sin to be gay," I said. But, his voice got louder and more aggressive as he insisted that this was not true. This brief dialog only went on for a few minutes until my smoke detector started going off, loudly interrupting his words. (I had forgotten to take the battery out of it when I began cooking, as the heat from the oven often sets off the alarm. I choose to think of it as divine intervention, though). As the old man paused from his rhetoric, searching my eyes to explain the loud alarm that was sounding off, his pause gave me a chance to terminate the futile discussion. I quickly announced that the alarm was my "Christian Detector" and I slammed the door.

I was angry, frustrated, insulted, disrespected, and

felt violated by the couple's presence as well as their "good word." However, for a brief moment in time, when the alarm first started going off, I saw the man as he was. His face was startled and he stopped talking just for that brief second. He became human. In that one moment, he was just a man, tired and old, but believed that he was doing the Lord's work by trying to save souls. We became just three human beings standing there, myself, the man and his wife. And in that very moment, I saw his humanity. He was not a threat just then and I knew he could not hurt me. I also knew that I did not want to hurt him. We were just two souls staring at each other, yearning for answers, believing our thoughts, and we were not enemies.

As quickly as the moment happened, though, it went away. The humanity of the situation and of the three human beings standing there was gone and our egos all returned to their rightful owners. Both of our defenses immediately went back up, our armor was back on, and we were on GO again. I have reflected on that brief moment of humanity that I witnessed and experienced since it happened. I wondered if he had the same sensation. Probably not, maybe so, but it doesn't really matter, I guess. My conclusion to all of this is that I want to remember that moment in time where I saw things from my spirit's point of view. I loved the feeling of that one second where we were human, equal, and both just trying to survive the best way we knew how. We were both living how we felt we should be living and were both doing what we felt we should do. I felt no fear at that time, no disrespect. In fact, I felt nothing personal but everything personal all at once because we were just spirits who were not connecting. Both of our egos, the man's and mine, came back so quickly that maybe he missed it. Or maybe my humanity did not show through my eyes and I still looked like the enemy to him. I will never know. But, I will always remember that brief moment of humanity that I felt and saw because I have to wonder what it would be like, what life would be like, if we always saw the humanity in each other and in all situations. That's the positive that I took from the whole experience, and I hope I will never be the same because of it.

YOU CAN BE RIGHT OR YOU CAN BE HAPPY

(And Expectations vs. Standards)

Being right feels good, but sometimes being happy feels better. When we are having an argument with someone on a topic that we disagree on, but we know for a fact that we are in the right about, we persist on trying to get the other person to see our point of view. We want that person to realize that their understanding or belief about the topic is wrong and our belief is correct. We sometimes feel this incessant need to educate them and have them admit that they are wrong about the topic being discussed. However, not all topics are black or white when discussing the right or wrong especially about a belief or opinion. Some of us don't give up the fight, though. We will go at it for hours, talking and talking, trying to make the other person see our point of view, so that we can be seen as right and we can feel even more right.

Enlightened people don't have this urgent need to be right or expect the other person to know/admit they are right and the other person is wrong. They are okay with people who aren't ready to see things differently yet. Enlightened people understand that everyone moves along their journey at their own pace, in their own time. They don't need others to recognize that they are right and they don't demand others to see or agree with their point of view. They don't need these things to be happy. They can be happy without people knowing that they are right about something, or anything, for that matter. But, enlightened people aside, sometimes we need to pick our battles wisely. We don't need to win every argument in order to be happy. In fact, sometimes it comes down to a decision, a choice. We can stay in the argument, knowing we are right, demanding that the other person agrees with us that we are right, OR we can agree to disagree and walk away happy. The sooner we believe that we don't need to be seen as right all the time in order to be happy, ironically, the happier we really will be. The less we expect from others, the happier we will be, too.

I believe that expectations are demands that you place onto others, which will eventually let you down and cause you pain. They can range from expecting people to say thank you or I'm sorry, to expecting people to adhere to your set of morals with how you expect to be treated by others. Presumptions almost demand a behavior from someone else. A change in them, perhaps. On the other hand, standards are your own set of rules or guidelines that you follow in the way YOU behave or treat others. Standards are also limits you have on what you will and will not tolerate or accept from others. To tell you not to have any expectations of others is **not** to say let them walk all over you or abuse you, because that is where standards come in. Standards do not really expect anything from other people. They don't place assumptions or demands for change onto others. They are your own moral code as to what you are willing to have in your life, what you are willing to accept from others, and what you are willing to put up with/tolerate.

The catch is that sometimes we have little choice in who we have in parts of our lives, like at work. That is where tolerance comes in. Tolerance doesn't expect you to lower your standards, but asks you to deal with it for the time being to get through the situation/circumstance, like having to be at work, around people who do not treat you with respect, etc. I believe that expectations come from our ego and from our attachments. Standards come from our spirit and won't let you down like expectations will. Standards are meant to empower you, help you find your voice, set your limits, and develop your own moral code for how you choose to live your life.

ARE YOU OUT OF YOUR MIND?

When we refer to someone who is "out of his/her mind," we are usually talking about someone who seems crazy, has a severe mental disorder, or someone who is just not "thinking." I believe that just the opposite can be true. I have found that for myself, I am most crazy when I am IN my mind. While imagination is great and dreams can be fun, the mind can also develop a darker reality inside itself. My mind, for example, is a dangerous place for me to be at times. It is a domain all its own where I get trapped in the swirling of thoughts, ideas, and premonitions. No matter how fast or how many times I drive my thoughts around the giant round track, I still end up nowhere or worse. I sometimes end up in a state of pondering where validity means nothing. It's just thoughts breeding more thoughts, questions that will never have answers here on this earth, making a rut into my very soul. The well is deep, my friends, and it's best not to dive in head first, because the more time you spend in that well, thinking about what you are going to do, the less time you have to actually do it.

If you *dwell in the well* on something long enough, it becomes your reality, at least in your head. Quite frankly, I don't come up with the best scenarios sometimes of how I think things are going to turn out. I find this is very hard because I have the notion that if I just think about something long enough (aka: worry/obsess), the answers will come, and that simply is just not true for me, all the time. Sure, I think I'd love to know what happens when we die, where do we really go or not go, what is it really all about, but I must learn to give up that false sense of control that I want so bad to have about these things and everything else.

To conclude this brief essay, I just want to say that I am going to try to stay out of my mind, at least some of the time, where my thinking cannot get the best of me. When we are *out of our minds,* we can experience things as they come, being totally present in the here and now. Stay in the present just for today, this hour, this minute, and bit by bit as this is occurring, maybe, just maybe, we can enjoy it. It's really about mindfulness vs. willfulness. When we are being mindful, we are being fully aware of the here and now. We focus all our attention on the present moment, thinking our thoughts, and feeling our feelings, then letting them go without getting stuck in judgment over them. Mindfulness is about letting your spirit guide you. On the other hand, when we are being willful, we are more close minded, stubborn, and it is our ego that is driving us. The ego of our mind will deliberately hold onto a belief despite reason and prevents us from moving forward on our journey. Staying in our ego state, trapped inside our own minds, prevents us from truly being present. We are all *up inside our heads,* obsessing about the past or worrying about the future, either way, we are missing the present. The term mindfulness can be misunderstood as having a mind that is full, but it means that we are allowing our spirit to keep us fully focused and aware of the here and now. When we do this, we appreciate life more, we recognize the small but important moments, and we are better able to experience life to the fullest. So, in this case, being out of our minds is really a wonderful thing.

"Let us not look back in anger nor forward in fear, but around in awareness."[17]
-James Thurber

OBSERVATION VS. JUDGMENT

As I was sitting in the dentist's office lobby waiting to be seen, there was also a boy, probably about the age of 15, sitting in the waiting room with me. There was no one else in the room to "people watch," so my eyes homed in on studying him. I figured his parent or guardian must be in with the dentist because the boy did not look old enough to drive there himself. He sat in a much-slumped position, staring at his iPhone, appearing quite depressed. If this were a doctor's office, I might have thought his loved one was undergoing serious surgery and he was updating their status on social media, because he looked so distraught. His body language yelled boredom, though, so I thought maybe he's just bored. After all, he was already waiting when I got there and checked in, so maybe he had been waiting a long time? Poor thing. His mom might be in the chair getting a root canal, and those things take time. He had ripped blue jeans on (that looked like they were purchased that way) and his eyes never left his phone. He would text something on it every now and again as he changed his slumped posture into a different, depressed position. His black t-shirt had a music band on it that I had never heard of and as I sat there studying him, I felt very old. Suddenly, I found myself judging him. What did he have to be depressed about? He had been on this earth maybe all of 15 years. Was his life that hard? My 46-year-old body secretly said to him, "You ain't seen nothing yet, boy." The sunlight from the waiting room window was cast upon him now and I decided that he was probably just spoiled. A lot of kids are these days. He was 15; did he really need an iPhone? Okay, maybe he bought it with saved up paper route money, but surely his parents bought it for him. What was happening to me? Why did my observation turn to judgement just then?

And then I remembered when I was 15 years old. I was severely, clinically depressed and when I tried to share this with my parents, I remember my father saying to me, "What do you have to be depressed about? You have nothing to be depressed about!" He didn't understand how clinical depression worked. He didn't know that with clinical depression, there often isn't an obvious, outward cause of it, such as an event or a situation. He didn't understand or know that clinical depression is biological and sometimes there's not an outside reason that people can see. I was diagnosed with bipolar disorder years after that, when I had finally decided to get help for my mental disorder because it was going to kill me if I didn't. So, then I felt bad, and rightfully so, as I was thinking about this young man sitting chairs away from me in the dentist's waiting room. Maybe he wasn't just being a typical teenager? He might very well have a chemical imbalance in his brain that he is either getting help for or is not aware of yet. "I'm sorry, young man. I'm sorry."

In analyzing the young boy, maybe 10 minutes had passed, which felt like an hour. Then the door to the outside opened and in walked a woman with a young girl. The mother checked in at the front desk and they both sat down across from me. The woman sat down, the girl plopped down and pulled out her Android device. This girl also appeared to be a teenager, maybe around the age of 14. She gave a heavy sigh and joined the teenage boy in the slumped position in her chair. Granted, the hard, wooden chairs weren't the most comfortable, but she looked tired and bored as soon as her butt met the wood. Either teenage depression is more widespread than I thought or I was just realizing and remembering what it was like to be a teenager. Most of them do look depressed, if you ask me, and maybe they are. I decided that I wasn't going to judge this time. Just purely observe.

Then, more memories came flooding back to me. I was not a happy teenager; maybe none of them are happy? The teen years are an incredibly hard age to survive, if you ask me. Mine was full of angst, as I am convinced that most of them are. If the hormone changes alone don't make you feel like you are drowning, then the peer pressure surely will. I have read many psychological studies that have determined that it is the age between 18-21 where an adolescent begins to think outside him or herself. Adolescents enter that very self-absorbed stage between 12-17 first, though, and unfortunately, some never grow past it. All of us know at least one adult who is so consumed with him/herself that it seems like they never consider other people's feelings. What pushes us past the stage of Erik Erikson's idea of development where the young person enters the identity vs. confusion stage? As teenagers, we must find our own identity that is separate from our parents, and we must start to form our own individual self. Then, as we continue to mature, we must think outside ourselves to a more global awareness of others and our surroundings. This should be in full force, I am guessing, from age 18 and beyond. I would imagine that there are many causes as to why young adults get stuck and do not move pass the self-awareness stage. Don't they always say we must learn to love ourselves before we can love others? Self-esteem must come first before we can have compassion for others.

So, I am still sitting in the waiting room with the two teens who were waiting on their guardians, and I can't help but analyze. It's just in my nature to do so. As I am studying these young creatures of sadness and discontent, I decided that I am old. There are days when my body has many aches, pains, and feels older than other days, but I have always considered my mind to be quite young. But, as I gazed upon the teenagers in the room with me, I felt old in my mind as well as in my body. Then, the outside door opened again and a hunched over elderly woman entered the room. She had a cane with her, but it must have only been for security's sake, because she was carrying it without it even touching the ground as she came into the room. She checked in and sat down on the other side of me, positioned the cane between her knees and clasped her hands together. She looked tired, but she didn't look depressed, and she did not produce any electronic device from her pocket or purse to keep her entertained. Suddenly, I didn't feel so old. This reminds me that life is mostly about perspective.

I have heard people say, in life, we regret more the things we didn't do, rather than the things we did do. I disagree with this statement even though I am guessing it was written/said to encourage people to get out there and live their life by taking chances and trying new things, before they get too old to be able to do them and end up with that kind of regret. I regret a lot more things that I did do rather than things that I didn't do. In my 46 years of life, I've survived crazy on numerous occasions, but I don't regret the times when I chose to get help, or even the times I was forced to get help. Despite how traumatic some of those times were, I don't regret it because that was part of the road, the journey I had to take to get where I am today. I *do* regret in the beginning, not taking my stays in the mental hospitals and my time spent with therapists more seriously, because maybe I would be farther along than I am now. Who's to say, though?

When I hear the saying, everything happens for a reason, I believe it's somewhat true, but I also believe that sometimes, the reason *things happen* is because of the poor choices we often make in life. However, I am not sure that I believe in the **spiritual belief** that everything happens for a reason. Sometimes bad things happen because there are *hurt people* out there who hurt other people. Sometimes things happen because of a causality: the relationship between cause and effect. But, to say that there is a definite reason, especially a spiritual or *God-intended* reason, for everything that happens, that I do not believe. They will tell me that sometimes we may never know the (God's) reason why certain things happen, but there's still a reason. If this is sincerely true, God truly is as cruel as I imagine Him to be. Of course, I am back to thinking about little babies who are burned with cigarettes, raped by their fathers, and left to bleed to death in a garbage dump somewhere. In my mind, in my opinion, there can be absolutely NO purposeful or good enough reason for God to allow that to happen in this world. I guess with even horrible events such as that, though, there still could be a human-based reason, like "some people are just truly fucked up." It's not a good or purposeful reason, but a reason nonetheless, therefore, a *cause* for it. Cause and reason are different, though, aren't they? My bottom line on this whole notion is that I must believe in coincidences. Things that sometimes seem connected, but are not. It doesn't comfort me to think that some things happen just randomly and for no reason or connection, but to even believe in theories like six degrees of separation just blows my mind. Maybe I am not far enough along in my journey yet for my brain to comprehend it.

But back to regret. There are poor choices I have made, many mistakes I have made, and just outright things that I have done consciously that I do regret. I feel like I have lived a life, though, *lifetimes* actually, and there's very little that I regret *not* doing. I've been to the Bahamas, Las Vegas, Put-In-Bay, Ohio, New Jersey, West Virginia, Canada, New York City, and Florida (many times), and the memories that my ECT brain allows me to recall are extremely valuable to me, because most of those trips were time spent with my mother, who is also my best friend. In the early 1990's when cassettes were still popular, before compact discs took over, I had two music cassettes of songs produced and recorded in a studio, which I actually wrote and sung. One of my songs was even played on the radio twice, and I even attempted to sell my cassettes in a local music store.

Much of this stuff, people who aren't close to me don't know. When I feel their judgmental eyes on me when I am using my food stamp card to buy some of my groceries, they don't know that I have a 4-year bachelor's degree in social work under my belt and that I started working at the age of

16. I worked a wide variety of jobs during high school, before college, during college, and after college. I worked with many different populations of people: people who suffer from mental illness, mentally challenged people, wayward and troubled children, the elderly, and brain injured people, in a variety of different settings. I have attempted numerous jobs of a wide variety throughout my life, and after years and years of trying to stay employed, sometimes lasting as long as 5 years at a job and sometimes only lasting 2 weeks, my mental illness has always, eventually prevented me from staying gainfully employed. I also tried to go back to college to get a different degree, to get a different type of job. In 2001, I attempted to get a massage therapist degree, and I did well for the first year and a half. I had one more semester to go before graduating and obtaining my degree when my bipolar disorder symptoms resurfaced so intensely that I had to withdraw from college and be hospitalized.

So, in 2006, I finally had to accept the limitations of my illness and unhappily had to surrender to needing financial government assistance. The government deemed me permanently disabled and I have, unfortunately, been on social security disability since that time. However, contrary to popular belief about people on government assistance, or even people on social security disability, I am honestly NOT lazy. I WANT to work. I WISH I could work. This has bothered me from the very first day I became officially mentally disabled and could not be gainfully employed any longer. I am now in the vicious cycle or trap of being on social security disability, having used up all my trial work period attempts, and deemed "permanently disabled." I am too afraid to even try to work again because if I attempt to work now, I would lose my meager but steady monthly income of SSD, and even worse, lose my health insurance that I receive through SSD. Then, if I failed at that next attempt at working at a job, I would have absolutely nothing. No income, no health insurance, and it would be extremely hard to get back on SSD at that point. I have written about this frustration in my first book, and I am probably mentioning it again in this book because I, unfortunately, care what people think about me. I know how judgmental many people can be about someone getting something that they aren't getting, or that they themselves must work for. To many, if you can't SEE the disability, then you DON'T have one, which is false.

I hesitated to put this particular essay in my book, because I do talk about it in my first book. But, I also realize that it's still a huge trigger for me, when I hear people judging others who receive food stamps, and/or are on welfare. People also judge those individuals who are not working and are on social security disability. Their judgments are harshest when they cannot SEE the disability of the person receiving the benefits or when they can't understand why the person is on social security disability. They suddenly become doctors who feel they can best diagnose others and they believe they are qualified to determine if a person should be receiving the benefits or not, all based on what they see. I admit I do get very defensive and always feel the need to state my case, justify and explain myself. I try to make people understand why I am on social security disability and honestly cannot stay gainfully employed. I am told by my loved ones who do understand that I don't need to explain or justify my situation to others, and that it doesn't matter what others think. I have come to realize that people are only going to understand and see things from their perspective, anyway. Yet, I am keeping this section in my book, because I know there are others who, like me, feel badly about themselves for needing assistance. I am not the only one who feels *less than* for not being able to work and for being on social security disability. One of the main reasons I write about and share how I feel is to attempt to help others, who might feel similarly, to **not feel so alone**. It feels worse when you believe you are the only one who thinks or feels the way you do. It isolates people and can lead to a deeper depression or shame. So, while I continue to defend my journey, I more importantly want to defend others who are struggling with their own journey. Please know that you honestly are *not* alone.

I have come to accept the unpredictability of my mental illnesses, how they can resurface out of nowhere and cause extreme debilitation in my life. But, what I still need to work on is no longer worrying about what others, especially the ones who know nothing about me, think of me. *I* KNOW I am not lazy. *I* know I try my best every day. *I* know I can have my mental illness go into remission and will be fine for even a couple of years, only to have it rear it's disgusting, ugly head, making me resort to psychiatric hospitalization and electroconvulsive therapy in hopes of staying alive. So, yes, I still need to work on not caring about what some people may think about me. I think I will probably always care to some extent, about what people think of me. There's probably no escaping that, because I care about what people think, in general, about anything. Knowing this about myself, I have changed my goal to reaching a point in my life where I still care about what people think, but I don't let it negatively affect me. That, to me, is truly what finding peace is all about. If you can be happy with who you are, with who you find on your journey to self-discovery, without allowing the negative influences, opinions, and beliefs of others to affect your peace, you are well on your way to enlightenment.

I try to focus less on my limitations and more on what I *can* do with the remainder of my life. I have been volunteering at the Red Cross for nearly 2 years now, and I enjoy that very much. I try to remember that some people simply cannot understand another person's journey or where that person is on her path, because they are not in that other person's shoes, walking that particular path.

"People take different roads seeking fulfillment and happiness. Just because they're not on your road doesn't mean they've gotten lost."[18] **- Dalai Lama XIV**

WHY WE CAN'T JUST "GROW UP!"

(An essay written in an attempt to answer your question of "What the hell is wrong with people?!)"

"The main problem with society is that children are having children."
- Melissa Ross

This essay is a theory on human behavior. Many times, people will say to me that they just don't understand other people and their actions. This essay is an attempt to explain that. I believe that the reason people behave badly or childishly is because they are still little children inside and are operating with the skills of a child. This book is not about excusing this type of behavior, nor is it about placing blame on our parents. If we were to blame our parents, we would have to also blame their parents and their parent's parents, and so on. I simply hope to explain a possible reason for people's behavior and offer suggestions on how to become more aware of the child who lives inside us, ultimately healing that child so we can become more mature, better adults.

I believe the main problem society has is that children are having children. I am not referring to the obvious 15-year-old children giving birth to babies without first being emotionally developed enough to handle it. My theory is that very few of us are emotionally equipped to raise and properly care for ourselves, let alone a child, because we are mentally and emotionally still children ourselves. The contention of this essay is to delve into the theory that none of us have truly "grown up," but instead, we are stuck in our child mode. Much research has been done concerning our child within, that part of us who still shares the characteristics of a child, but I think Sigmund Freud explained it best when he referred to our superego, ego, and id. I realize many people are not fans of Freud, and therefore may not see the validity of his studies, but few can dispute that we all act a little childish at times. I started out wanting to title this essay, *Stuck In The Id*, but realized many are not familiar with the notion of id, so I am going to attempt to describe it in a condensed version here.

To understand the idea of being "stuck in the id," we must first understand what the "id" is. Freud coined the term when he explained that the human psyche is made up of three parts: The id, the ego, and the superego[19]. The super ego is like your inner parent, your conscience. It's the part of you that tells you what you should and shouldn't do (what is right and wrong). It's the moral part of us that develops due to ethical and moral restraints placed on us by our parents, guardians, and society. It is our highest part of our inner nature. Freud's ego is based in reality and would be considered our inner adult. It differs from the superego in that it's not based on morals, but reason. The ego realizes that people have wants and needs, and that being impulsive and/or selfish can hurt us and others. The bottom level is the most basic of the three levels and is the most primitive. It is called the id and doesn't concern itself with reality or the needs and wants of others, only its own gratifications.

According to Freud, we are born with our id[20].

Transanalysists would call this part of us "the child" in the three-part explanation of our psyche of parent, adult, and child. The id has no morals, nor reason, just desires on the most innate level. Dr. Lee Baer wrote a book called *"The Imp of the Mind"* to indulge a pathology of this, but I'm not talking so much about a mental illness of our id, just the basic exploration of how even the healthiest of the ids can drive us and keep us stuck in our child mode. In many ways, I believe we are stuck in this childlike id part of us. Some of us are better able to keep our id in check, but we are all still vulnerable to our id and its motivations. We have all behaved immaturely as adults at some point in our lives over some certain circumstance. Some of us seem to behave more childishly than others, but at least we all can say we've experienced the part of us that just "took over" at some point, in dealing with a stressor or situation, and later we were embarrassed at how we acted.

According to Freud, when we revert to a state of being, like that of a child, it's called regression[21]. To put it simply: when under stress, we regress (digress). This is a defense mechanism of ours to protect our ego. When thoughts move from the conscious to the subconscious, they can get stuck there. We become fixated on the thought and become unable to control unacceptable impulses to deal with the discomfort of the fixation. It is my belief that if we do not deal with these fixations, we will not heal and will forever be at the mercy of our inner child, especially when under stress. I believe you must "deal to heal." If we do not work on healing these fixations, they become stronger, and turn into addictions. Our unsatisfactory reality becomes unfavorable and we search for an escape to avoid the pain of it.

This is where we can become alcoholics, drug addicts, sex addicts, food addicts, obsessive-compulsives, and our fixations become our main focus of our lives. This is all in an attempt to comfort our inner child and calm our id. If we continue to ignore the need to heal each of our children within, we will not be mature enough, mentally and emotionally, to raise a healthy child in this society; ones who have the necessary adult skills to cope with life's stressors. And the cycle will continue.

I believe Dr. Christopher L. Heffner, a licensed psychologist, explained it best in his article, *Id, Ego, Superego, and the Unconscious in Psychology 101* from Allpsych.com[22]. He stated that *"in a healthy person, according to Freud, the ego is the strongest, so that it can satisfy the needs of the id, not upset the superego, and still take into consideration the reality of every situation. If the id gets too strong, impulses and self-gratification take over a person's life. If the superego becomes too strong, the person would be driven by rigid morals, would be judgmental and unbending in his interactions with the world. The ego tries to maintain control over all of this, but it's my opinion that our id is usually the one behind the wheel."*

Human beings are both adaptable and resilient, as well as fragile and easily wounded. The human body can be cut or wounded and heal (regenerate), but it cannot grow back a missing body part. You may have heard the phrase that kids are so resilient/adaptable, and on the surface, they do seem to be. However, we are just recently getting more advanced at realizing just how delicate our psyche is, especially a child's, which is still developing. If you don't believe this, just look at the sales of Ritalin (a medication for attention deficient hyperactivity disorder) or turn on the TV and wait for the commercial of the latest medication for depression. With all of the drug companies getting rich off our illnesses of the mind, maybe we are finally learning that humans aren't so resilient and adaptable, especially concerning children, especially when dealing with our id.

> *"If you try to just "put on your big girl panties and deal with it," without first healing your inner child, you are just going to end up shitting your pants."*
> -Melissa Ross

I feel that the "suck it up" method does not work. Some people believe we just have to "pull ourselves up by our bootstraps" sometimes, in dealing with unpleasant things. While that theory may be somewhat true, the harsh line of thinking to yell at ourselves to **"JUST GROW UP!"** will eventually backfire, almost every time. To put it bluntly, if you try to just "put on your big girl panties and deal with it" without first having compassion enough to heal your inner child, you are just going to eventually end up shitting your pants. In other words, you can't demand a feather to catch a bowling ball. It just can't be done, because no matter how much you try to *will* it into capability, a feather cannot hold the weight of a bowling ball. It's really that simple. If you don't have the skills to do something, to deal effectively with something or a situation, you will not be able to do it, at least not for long, no matter how much you yell at yourself to "suck it up."

Many people in our society have that brutal theory to beat ourselves up when we can't do something, and to make fun of the "touchy-feely" people who believe in having compassion for ourselves and others. "Might doesn't always equal right." To try and force ourselves to mentally and emotionally grow up is how I feel we got ourselves into this problem state of being in the first place. We've yelled at our real children to "grow up!" just like our parents yelled at us, and how their parents yelled at them. You cannot yell something into existence, no matter how much you pull up those bootstraps, no matter how big of big girl panties you put on, and no matter how much you try and force it. Just as beating a child doesn't teach him right from wrong, it just teaches him to be sneakier and not get caught the next time. *Willing* our child within to behave, to stay inside us always, and to not act out, just doesn't work.

We must have compassion with ourselves. We must also have compassion for our parents, because as they were raising us, they too were just children (inside). Parents and guardians are people, too, and they are fallible human beings, just like we all are. As adults, we can look at our parents, see their faults, and on an intellectual level understand that most parents did the best they could. I am not excusing their behavior or trying to reason away why some parents abuse and neglect their children. It's just not helpful at this point to play the blame game. I highly recommend therapy for adult children who had toxic parents, but the point of this essay is not to place responsibility on anyone else, but to heal our inner child, so we can live more productively and harmoniously. The only person who can truly do this for us is ourselves. We must first recognize and "own" our inner child, understand its needs and wants, then work on healing him/her. This process definitely takes time, but can lead to a fuller and happier life in the long run. As we progress and heal our inner child, we will be able to see that our parent's behavior towards us as we were growing up were just signs of their inner child needing to heal from their parents. This cycle of unhealed patterns will continue until we are able to heal. This essay isn't about growing up, though. It's about evolving, transforming, and finding yourself; over and over and over again.

"People don't grow up. They just learn
how to act in public."[23]
-Bryan White

So, if none of us truly grows up, then why don't we appear to act like children all the time? This is because some of us have been able to develop a certain awareness as to how to act like an adult in public, therefore not revealing our inner child. No one can do this all the time, though, because the id is a very powerful force with which to contend. Most us, the functioning part of society, have learned how to play the games. However, when we look at these actions, we can still see the childish reversion in each game's nature. At the very core of these games, there are

still the dynamics of a child. Dr. Eric Berne wrote a fascinating book about these games called *Games People Play*[24], in which he describes these childish games that adults play with each other to get what they want. These are also known as mind games, power games, or head games, in which we struggle for one *upmanship* through passive-aggressive behavior. I highly recommend Dr. Berne's book on this subject to better understand this behavior.

Sigmund Freud also explained why adults play these

childish games in his studies of human behavior[25]. I feel in order to understand people, we must look at the very things that a child does want, and, more importantly, needs. So, what does the id want? What commonalities are we born with that drive us? On the most basic level, we are motivated by pleasure and pain. We move towards and do what brings us pleasure, and we try to avoid or escape what causes us pain. A healthier superego or inner parent will have guidelines or morals as to the right or socially acceptable way to achieve happiness (pleasure) and avoid pain. A healthy ego, the adult within, will reason with ourselves as to the pros and cons of achieving happiness by socially acceptable means, such as working hard, learning a trade, acting appropriately to get what we want or what we think we need. The question, then, is why do we sometimes (more often than not for some) get stuck in the id? Well, what does a child need and want as he/she is growing up? I'll refer to Abraham Maslow's *Hierarchy of Needs*[26] to illustrate this. When we are born, we can do basically nothing for ourselves. Sure, we can eat and poop, but someone must feed us and clean up after us. Someone must teach us right from wrong. Someone must tell us the socially acceptable rules of behavior. In my opinion, this is the only viable example of how a child can be considered "born a sinner." We are truly born ignorant of society's rules and agreements. All we know is what our id wants and needs.

It's true that "normal is just a setting on a washing machine," in that, it's what each society deems as acceptable. A majority group of people get together, form a group or society, and agree on what's right and wrong for that society. The society comes to an agreement on proper actions, behaviors, thoughts, and feelings, then calls that normal. Anything opposing that majority agreement is called abnormal, weird, strange, and/or socially unacceptable. Societies around the world differ on what's normal, based on what that society needs to survive and its culture. One society may find it morally apprehensible to murder, and make it against the law. Another society will have total justification for a couple to kill their firstborn child if it's not a male. Is one agreement right and the other wrong? That would depend on the culture or society in which you live.

Our basic needs as children are ones we cannot give ourselves. The first needs are food, clothing, and shelter. We do not charge a child with indecent exposure when we find him with his diaper off. But, if someone hasn't moved passed their id's nature to be naked and he exposes himself as an adult, he will be charged with a crime. Maslow's *Hierarchy of Needs* are what every adult needs to be fully actualized, but what do children need? Are these needs the same as our adult needs? If none of us are truly adults, but still children on the inside, then these needs/wants are the same, just obtained through different acceptable and unacceptable ways. No one can dispute our first set of needs, the physical ones, such as: the need for air, food, water, sleep, exercise (and for adults, sex is included here). The next set of needs are our emotional needs: the need for praise (attention), love (comfort), trust (safety), security, feeling "okay inside" (validity) and self-fulfilled. The third set of needs, as described by Maslow, are our social needs: the need for companionship and friendship, good dialog/communication, and a sense of belonging to a peer group. We also have intellectual needs, such as: the need for challenging thoughts, ability to read, ability to learn something new, and mind stimulation. Creative needs include: the need to express yourself in the way you desire, anything that allows you to feel imaginative, and inspired (stimulated). The last set of needs would be our spiritual needs, such: the need for quiet inside our heads, harmony and consistency of our thoughts, a need to want to know and believe in a higher spiritual power greater than ourselves, which increases our awareness and sensitivity to the greater things about life and the afterworld. Not everyone feels the need to believe in something or someone greater than themselves, though. These people would need the right to choose not to believe in a higher power, but a belief in one's own self is essential for growth, to move beyond childhood and move into adulthood.

The id is not necessarily bad, just like a child is not born evil, just ignorant. I realize it's a widespread belief among Catholics and possibly other religions that a child is "born into sin," but I believe we, as humans, have created sin, defined it, and brought the idea of it into being with our morals, regulations, laws, and rules. We've created sin much like we named and created "God," thus determining the balance between good and evil. We didn't so much as give birth to our Creator. He/She/It is what created us and decided to start the human race. Something caused the big bang, or breathed the first breath of life into the protozoa, the ape, the cave man, whatever theory of creation or evolution you ascribe to. It's more that we defined God, named Him, limited Him, and put Him into a state of which we could understand Him (or Her or It).

The id is our most primitive part of us. It's primordial and is our child within. As I mentioned, we are all basically motivated through pleasure and pain. We try to do the things that cause us pleasure and avoid the things that cause us pain. And the id wants what it wants, without conscience or reason, so what makes some of us better to control this imp in public? I know some of us who would rather die than be caught picking particles out of their nasal cavity in public, but I bet most of us have picked our nose in private. However brief and however you justify it, an itch, whatever- we've all at least blown our nose in private. It's the superego that tells you it's wrong and gross to pick your nose in public. It tells us that you will disgust others and end up with no friends, or to coin a phrase from the movie, "*Carrie,*" they are at least "all gonna laugh at you.[27]" It's our *ego* that tells us picking our nose in public is just not socially acceptable, besides that's how germs are spread. But, it's our *id* that cares about none of that. The *id* picks it's nose because there's discomfort of some sort and it feels good to eliminate the itch or bothersome irritation. Why do you think so many kids have to be taught not to put their fingers up their nose, especially in public? Because kids aren't born with reason or what the rules are as to what's socially acceptable and what is not.

The next step in our drives and decisions towards pleasure and away from pain is the "fight, flight, or freeze syndrome." When confronted with opposition to our need for pleasure and our avoidance of pain, we act accordingly to obtain what we want (and don't want). If we feel the opposition is too threatening, we become afraid and withdraw or flee the situation (back down). If we think we can conquer the opposition, we do not take flight, but stand and fight, instead. Fighting takes courage and strength.

Each child within has a different degree of that, depending on what was instilled in him when he was younger, by his parents or guardians. It was just recently that some psychologists have added the freeze option to the fight or flight theory. It was finally recognized that there is one other option to choose from between staying and fighting or retreating and taking flight. Sometimes a person gets so overwhelmed by opposition that they become figuratively immobile and are unable to choose to fight or take flight. The freeze option can also happen to a person in which they simply are incapable of taking any action and therefore *freeze* in the face of a challenge. Their brain becomes too overwhelmed to make a healthy decision between the two. Many people with mental health disorders know this freeze position all too well. Often professional help is needed if a person experiences this freeze position more frequently than just occasionally. This person is not equipped to handle becoming overwhelmed and their id has somehow, in some way, been damaged to the point where choosing a healthy fight or flight response is often impossible to do. If an adult chooses to stay and fight for what he wants or needs, this is where the game playing begins. But first, let's discuss childlike behavior. Of course, each of these points may not be true for every single child in the world. These points are mentioned in general, and are listed as common, basic attributes of children.

1. Children feel the need for instant gratification. They want things "now!" and they don't want to wait, nor do they understand the positive effects of working for something they obtain.

2. Children have a sense of entitlement. I call this the "Mine!" syndrome, where a young child thinks every toy is his or should be his. Since they basically need things handed to them, that is how they believe they should get everything.

3. Children are very self-absorbed. It's all about "me" (or them) in their thinking. Based on the studies of children, it is not until the age of 15 that a young person begins to think outside himself and consider others in the equation. The world is centered on and around them and they cannot commiserate with how others may feel or consider what others think about any given situation.

4. Children believe in having things done their way. If other children are not playing the game according to the child who is in possession of the "ball" that child decides to just quit, take his ball and go home. It's their way or the highway, so to speak.

5. Children do not know how to self-soothe properly and are always seeking comfort from outside sources, such as from their parents.

6. Children do not know how to problem-solve, and therefore do not have the skills to figure things out on their own, but seek help from their peers.

7. Children do not know how to take responsibility for their actions, and believe that a problem situation is someone else's fault. They do not take accountability for their part of the problem situation, and blame everything and everyone else. Since young children cannot take accountability for things, they believe

the situations they get in are someone else's fault as well.

8. Children are very vengeful and they like to get even with a child who has hit them, stole something from them, or has otherwise have harmed them.

9. Children lie and do not understand the value or need to tell the truth. They will lie, especially to minimize or eliminate their part if they get into trouble, and they will try to get other children into trouble by blaming them.

10. Children believe they are invincible and can never die. Therefore, they are risk takers, and do not believe anything bad can happen to them.

Have you ever seen any of these child characteristics played out in any adult behavior? Adults play a lot of childish, mental games with each other, too. One only must be a fly on the wall in an office setting and watch the dynamics of the workers, and how they interact with each other to understand that adults still possess and utilize their child like characteristics. We find some of this behavior in everyone we know and meet, even in our loved ones, and even in ourselves. Most of us are all basically just children inside, who have not grown up. So, do any of you readers still feel that most us couldn't possibly be stuck in Freud's id? I think if this weren't true, we wouldn't have crimes committed every few seconds worldwide, we wouldn't have overcrowded jails, and we wouldn't need selected men and women called police to enforce society's acceptable and agreed upon rules. To some extent, we are all just children, running wild.

Someone who never has problems with his or her id would always be reasonable, realistic, responsible, mature, competent, decisive, dependable, self-aware, able to accept and process criticism appropriately, and would be fully self-actualized.... all the time. They would never feel vulnerable, insecure, dependent, immature, or be fearful of rejection. Do you know anyone like that? Maybe you do. There are people out there who have enough self-awareness to realize and accept their id. These people heal and nurture their inner child daily, and are the most emotionally healthy of adults. It is possible for you to do this as well, but it takes awareness, consistency, and persistence. Just as a child in real life needs and wants things every day, so does your inner child. The more we are aware of these things, the happier our inner child will be, and our adult self can maintain control in our lives.

On an intellectual level, we can understand all of this, but please remember that your id works on a very emotional level. Emotions can't be reasoned away. They must be acknowledged, accepted, felt, and finally released. Your parents may have been the best parents in the entire world, but your inner child still responded in some way to your parent's mistakes, which arose from their own need to heal and your inner child hasn't forgotten those feelings. When you were little you didn't have a lot of power in your world and were dependent on the care of others to provide for you and to love you. The people who raised you may have met all of these needs, but maybe they didn't. It's even possible that they did, but you were still sad, angry, frustrated, and felt unheard. Those feelings never went away. All the feelings we felt as a child, growing up, are still there, inside you somewhere. This is what our id holds onto, what it knows, and what dictates our adult behavior at times.

There are so many good books out there on how to heal your inner child that it would be redundant of me to explain how in this essay. I basically want to encourage people to become aware of what may be going on inside themselves, and others as to why we behave the way we behave. In an article from Brighthill.net called, *Healing Your Inner Child*[28], Asha Hawkesworth asks your inner child the following 6 things, regarding what your inner child may be feeling. These are:

1. Do you ever feel unheard and that your thoughts, feelings, and opinions were not heard or respected?
2. Do you ever feel guilty, as though you could never please your parents or make them happy? Or perhaps your parents divorced and somehow you feel that was your fault?
3. Do you ever feel abandoned? Maybe you lost a parent through death or divorce and you may still be grieving a lost relationship with that parent.
4. Do you feel sad, deep down, like you were afraid to be yourself because your parents might not approve of that person? Did you feel that you had to do or be certain things to be loved?
5. Do you feel unworthy, like you could do not right, that you could never win? Or felt that you were stupid, ugly, or not as good as other people?
6. Do you feel angry when you feel like you are not being heard? Did you not feel loved for who you really are, or didn't feel safe?

Hawkesworth states that "if any of these feelings push your buttons, take note. Your inner child is telling you something, and you have work to do. If you don't heal these feelings, they will run your life.[29]"

Erik Erikson wrote several books in his attempt to describe development that occurs throughout the lifespan. He explains 8 stages of psychosocial development[30], and if we did not get what we needed in the first 4 stages: infancy to adolescence: (ages birth to 18 years), we could have problems with our inner child as well. The basic conflict in our first stage of life (birth to 18 months), we learn *trust vs. mistrust.* If a child at this age develops a healthy sense of trust when caregivers provide reliability, care, and affection, the child learns to trust. A lack of this will lead to mistrust. The second stage, which is early childhood (ages 2 to 3 years old), is where the child needs to develop a sense of personal control over physical skills and a sense of independence. This leads to feelings of autonomy. If a child does not learn this, the results are *shame and doubt.* Preschool years, ages 3 to 5, are where the child explores and learns *initiative vs. guilt.* A child at this stage needs to begin asserting control and power over his environment, which leads to a sense of purpose. Children who try to exert too much power experience disapproval, resulting in a sense of guilt. Children who are in the age range of 6 to 11 years old are in the school age years, and this is the 4th stage of development according to Erikson. The 4th stage represents *industry vs. inferiority,* in that a child needs to cope with new social and academic demands. Success at this stage leads to a sense of competence while failure results in feelings of inferiority. The last of the first 5 stages of psychological development in children is the adolescence stage" ages 12-18. This is called the *identity vs. role confusion* stage where teens need to develop a sense of self and personal identity. Success with this leads to the ability to stay true to yourself, while failure results on role confusion and a weak sense of self. There are 3 more stages in Erikson's psychological development, however the first 18 years of life, in my opinion, is where the child forms his or her personality, develops the skills to survive, and does the most important learning in order to grow up to be an adult. Erikson may disagree, but regardless, the point here is if we do not have success at these stages of childhood development, we can get stuck in them. These unmet needs end up still being an issue for us when we are adults.

Whether you believe in Freud's fixations where we get stuck in the *oral, anal, phallic, latent, and* genital stage or you believe in Erikson's basic conflicts in his 8 psychological stages of development, or some other known psychologist's research, or you believe none of it, there are still times when we see people behaving in such immature ways as adults, it's easy to at least consider that we adults maybe have not learned what we needed to learn as children. Maybe we have not gotten what we needed as children and these needs continue to play out throughout our adult lives.

"It's never too late to have a happy childhood." [31]
-Tom Robbins

Of course, we cannot literally go back in time and relive or recreate our childhoods. However, if we acknowledge the child who still lives in us, pay attention to its ongoing needs and heal it, we are able to let it out to play once in a while.

Healing your inner child is important if you want to live life to its fullest. Unfortunately, we suppress and discourage our child within and if it is not nurtured or given free expression sometimes, it suffers and acts out inappropriately. Your inner child is the sum of your emotional past, resulting from dealing with many events, incidents and emotions that are unresolved negative influences.

Everyone has the ability within themselves to be happy. This happiness lies within our inner child. When the inner child is nurtured and at peace, we are able to release negativity appropriately. Healing your inner child is an ongoing process as well along your journey to find yourself, which everyone needs to go through if they want to live life to its fullest and be happy. When you are dysfunctional in one or more areas of your life, the first place you should look is inward. A wounded inner child can lead to several problems in adult life, such as the inability to maintain normal relationships as well as a constant state of anxiety and depression. Many people who become codependent or turn to drugs and alcohol for help have done so in attempt to compensate for their wounded inner child. Your inner child is your source of creativity, joy and energy. Those who allow the *child within* them to have expression throughout their lives achieve an inner peace and emotional wellbeing. After you recognize and acknowledge your own *child within* along your path, try to make friends with him/her. There are countless books on how to heal our inner child. Choose the one that seems best for you and start your own process of healing. I believe if we do this, our relationships will improve, and we will finally be able to stop self-destructive behaviors that are holding us back from fulfillment. We can get unstuck and stop our id from running wild.

If we understand that other people along their own journey also get stuck in their id and are really just children acting out, we can better understand human behavior as well. As annoying as a screaming child is in a grocery store, we must understand that when others act out and behave immaturely, it's their wounded inner child that is screaming for help. Children are innocent and pure, but they also have needs. If we can learn to have compassion for other people's inner children as well as compassion for our own inner child, we may be able to tolerate it when other adults behave childishly. Just as there's no point in yelling at a child, there is no benefit to yelling at an adult whose id is acting out. It reminds me of a cute cartoon I saw once of a dog barking, and his owner yelling loudly at him to stop. In the dog's thought bubble, it read, "Cool! Now we are both barking!" The next time a family member or coworker is getting on your nerves by acting childishly, see their wounded child who lives within them who just wants attention because it has been repressed and hurt for so long. This compassionate approach to others can lead to getting less irritated, and can give insight to why people act the way they do. It might just answer your question of "What the hell is wrong with people?!," too.

There is hope in awareness to finally be happy in life. I believe this lies within the awareness, acknowledgement, and understanding that most of us are stuck in our id. The most important relationship in your life is the one you have with yourself, because in the end, it's all you have. Develop a good relationship with yourself along your journey to find yourself, because you will be with you for the rest of your life. Once you have been through the healing of your inner child, the result is greater happiness, and more spiritual and emotional wellbeing to continue your ongoing self-discovery journey. So, what are you waiting for? Your id is calling you.

EXISTENCE GOES ON

There are many sayings that I can't stand. These sayings include: *suck it up, get over it, put on your big girl panties and deal with it, pull yourself up by your bootstraps,* and other harsh statements that I hear people say to each other. I don't like these sayings because I feel that they are demeaning ways to minimize a person's feelings, and what that person might be going through. It doesn't matter if these people add that they are saying these things *out of love.* These statements are not only cruel and unfair, but unrealistic, as well. Some people may not even realize that these sayings can further hurt a person who is suffering, but many people who tell other people these things think they know exactly what they are doing when they say them. They believe that the person who reveals that they are struggling needs to just *toughen up,* and perhaps even *stop whining about it.* I can't stress enough how damaging it is to say these things. The belief that everyone CAN, in fact, be stronger, if they only chose to be is simply unrealistic, and often untrue. Unfortunately, some people think that everyone is born with the same coping capabilities, the same mental capacities for stress, and that if the person saying these hurtful statements can *do it* (meaning handle his stress, deal with what is bothering him, or be able to effectively let a thought or feeling go), then the person he is telling this unhelpful advice to should be able to *do it,* as well. We are all different, though, in our mental capacities, our stress tolerance levels, and our abilities to overcome diversity, and it is unfair to expect someone else to have your same exact potential to deal with problems.

Also, a person truly does not know what another person is going through unless they walk in their exact shoes. Notice that I didn't say walk their exact path. First, it would be impossible to walk another person's exact path, because even though you might have had a very similar thing happen to you, or be in a situation or circumstance that you think is identical, it is not. It cannot be exactly the same, because every situation is at least a little bit different. You couldn't walk in another person's exact *shoes*, either, even if you wanted to, because every person's interpretation, reality, perception, and way of dealing with things is usually a *lot* different.

Then, there are people who just don't have any compassion for other people, and will say the previously mentioned harsh statements to someone else basically because they just don't care enough to want to even try to understand where the other person might be coming from. Regardless of the intent of the saying, though, I think it really is best just not to give this judgmental, unhelpful advice to someone else. I honestly believe that in most cases, if not all, people really are doing the best they can with what they are given. If we all adopted that attitude, it would be a more peaceful place, and people would be less annoyed by each other, too.

There are two phrases I also do not like, that do not fit into the categories that I just talked about. These might even be worse things to say to someone else. These sayings are "everything is going to be alright." and "life goes on." I feel that these might possibly be even worse statements to say to someone else, because they are just LIES. Some things WILL still *matter in five years,* and everything is never going to be completely okay. That's just an unrealistic promise. Most of the time that people say this to someone else, the intent is to give comforting reassurance, or to calm a person down, which, on the surface, does seem loving and caring.

I do have to confess that I take things more seriously and literally than many other people do. I know that I am highly sensitive to things, as well. I can admit that, so that does have to be taken into consideration, but I still feel the need to warn people who say these things to other people to just be careful. These sayings may feel appropriate at the time and they very well might be, in the short term of things, but I also know that I am not the only one who could be hurt by hearing these things, in the long run. For example, for some, *life* **doesn't** *go on.* I would hope that no one would ever say to a person suffering with terminal cancer, "oh well, life goes on." I realize that this is an extreme example, but I still use it because while the world will still turn, and reproduction on earth will continue, some individual lives do not go on or continue.

Metaphorically speaking, sometimes people's lives turn into existences for a period, or even indefinitely, when they experience a tragic event, such as a death of a child, a devastating divorce, and the loss of identity from a variety of reasons. To tell someone who is experiencing a great amount of stress, that life will go on is often just not comforting to hear. It's like saying "what you are going through or have just been through might be awful, but guess what? In the big scheme of things, the world doesn't care, it will still turn. The sun will still rise tomorrow whether you do or not." By this point, you can probably gather that one of my biggest pet peeves is minimizing what someone else is going through. Please, if you want to be loving towards people and be a part of enhancing peace in this world, just be aware and careful of what you say to people. Thoughts should include feeling, and feelings should include thought.

THE BIRTH OF DUKE ULYSSES HUNTER

(My Alter Ego)

It just wouldn't be right if I didn't at least dedicate a short chapter/essay on Duke Ulysses Hunter. In fact, he insisted on it. I created the character of Duke a couple years ago when I was making home videos to send to my cousin, Jennifer, who had moved away to Florida. I missed her so much, and just made up Duke to make her laugh. Then, Duke went kind of dormant for a while, but he resurfaced, and became as big as life during last year's presidential race.

Duke is my alter ego (more like my "alter id") who decided to come out again in my personality because I simply couldn't handle the outrageous things that were happening during that political time when lines were clearly dividing people. Duke is a male character who is pretty much the epitome of a stereotypical, ignorant, redneck hillbilly. He is just about the opposite of who I really am on every level. I further created Duke's style and personality to be goofy and fun-loving, too, and started creating Duke videos to post on my social media page. It's not so much that Duke makes fun of other people, but that he makes fun of himself, and prides himself on his ignorance.

Believe it or not, understand it or not, Duke helps me cope. He is my outlet and release in response to an increasingly crazy world. When I put on that mustache and hat, and start talking in my Duke voice, it's almost like I become him. I'm not talking about having a split personality, but Duke does post a ton of videos when I become manic. On the surface, you might think he says some offensive and inappropriate things, but deep down, he really does have a heart, and is lovable in nature. After I was brave enough to post the first couple of Duke videos that I made to post on social media, I noticed that some of my online friends really enjoy the videos. Whether people can identify with Duke or just find him funny, the feedback I got from those first couple of videos was all the fuel I needed to make more.

I admit, I look completely ridiculous when I am dressed up in my Duke attire, but I have always been one to do pretty much anything for a laugh, even since I was a small child. The more people found my Duke videos to be funny and made them laugh, the more videos I created, until Duke finally now has his own Facebook page, which is a page linked to my own, so I can keep track of his shenanigans. He does seem to have a mind of his own sometimes! I really enjoy creating the Duke videos because I really enjoy making people laugh, or at least smile. One smile or chuckle can change a person's whole mood, and brighten their day. So, it's a win-win because through Duke I get to comically vent my frustrations with certain things in life, and at the same time there's an opportunity to try to make someone's day.

I truly encourage everyone to create their own alter ego personality to help them get through the craziness that life can throw at us sometimes. It's really about making fun of your own self, too, and when you can do that….no one else can do it better.

He who laughs, lasts.
(Old proverb)

THERE AND BACK AGAIN[32]

(Not your average *Hobbit's* journey)

One of the most helpful things I have learned along my journey so far is that, "the more I know, the more I realize I don't know." What I mean by that is, the more experiences I have, and more the more things that I learn... the more I realize that there is so much more to experience, and learn. With this entire book being said, I am fine with it if you choose to think that it's all bullshit. That's the glory about other people's thoughts, feelings, beliefs, and opinions; you can take them or leave them. If what I have said in this essay doesn't "sink in" with you, doesn't "speak to you," or isn't a good enough answer to your question as to why many people are assholes, that's okay. Maybe you will find better beliefs, better answers, along your own journey of finding yourself. I spoke of other people's behaviors because sometimes when looking at others, we are often looking at ourselves. I believe we as human beings have many more commonalities than differences. What we see in ourselves, we can often see in others, and what we see in others, whether we want to admit it or not, we often see in ourselves. In other words, in finding yourself there, you also find others. In finding others, we also find ourselves.

Often it seems like life comes around in full circle. We end up at square one at what we think is the end of our journey. Some of us may feel that all we do is go around in circles, but I don't think that is entirely true. Just as you can't touch the same water in a river twice, each time we feel like we've come full circle, we, are in fact, at least a little bit different than when we began the journey. We are changed by our experiences, our interactions with others, our gaining of knowledge, and are we changed through our healing.

There's a saying that goes something like, "*Those who cannot remember the past are condemned to repeat it*"[33], and that sucks when you have a memory like mine. But, I choose to look at it more like we continue to make the same mistakes, until we learn from those mistakes. We continue to experience the same, or similar, things in life until we learn the lesson from it. We meet people for a reason, usually to learn something from them, or for us to teach them something, and we have people leave our lives for reasons. Sometimes the reason is simply because you learn that a certain person is toxic to you, and you use good self-care by removing them from your life.

On our journey to finding ourselves, we can feel like we are going in that circle, or back to square one, the beginning. This makes me think about when I was admitted to the eating disorder unit of the psychiatric hospital, because they didn't have any beds anywhere else. I did not have an eating disorder at that time, but shortly after I was released from the hospital to continue the ECT treatments on an outpatient basis, I developed an eating disorder. Coincidence? I admit it is ironic, however, I don't believe there's any correlation to it. As mentioned, after I was finished receiving the ECT treatments, more of my sexual trauma came to the surface, and had to be dealt with. Having to discuss the rape again, and the sexual abuse that occurred for those two years prior to the rape, stirred up the emotions of me feeling powerless, and not in control. Anyone who has suffered from an eating disorder, or has a loved one dealing with such, knows that restricting your eating is a way to feel like you have power and control over yourself again. I suddenly started not liking the way I looked, maybe because I subconsciously felt like that hideous trash, because of the sexual abuse. I became extremely weird with my eating habits, only eating a tuna fish sandwich and baked chips every day, 5 days a week, for well over a year, and lost a good bit of weight. It made me feel good to be in control again, and I would become extremely upset in a most exaggerated way if anyone tried to make me eat anything else, or even OFFERED me other food. It became quite a problem for me by the time my weight got down to 112 lbs. It was maddening torture in my brain to realize and admit I now had an eating disorder, but enough of my loved ones kept insisting that this was a huge problem, and I finally accepted that, and dealt with it in therapy. Now, I feel like I am at a more normal weight. I'd still like to weigh less, but I don't feel the incessant need to deprive myself of food to get there.

If you would like to look at your journey in mathematical terms, the square root of one is one, so when you feel like you are back to square one on your journey of finding yourself, you are left with ONE (yourself). However, try not to focus on being *the cheese* that I previously mentioned, or get depressed because we basically come into this world alone, and we go out of it alone. That's not my point that I am trying to make, and I certainly don't want you to become dispirited after reading my book. It's important to remember, though, that YOU really are the most important person to take along on your path. In fact, you can't do it without you. Once we learn to be okay with ourselves, we become okay with where we are at, even at each beginning of our continual journey. Once this happens, it makes it easier, not easy, but easier, to find yourself. Once you know who you are at each beginning, it also becomes easier to decide who you want to be, and who it is that you actually want to find. Awareness (acknowledgement), acceptance, compassion for self, and perseverance are all key elements which you will need along your quest as well.

You may have heard the saying, "the purpose of life is a life of purpose,"[34] which I love, because, it's a circular statement that hopefully illustrates the whole point that we don't walk our paths in a straight line, but in a type of spiral or circle. However, I believe that our reason for being here is not only to live a life that's purposeful, but to learn to love each other, and help each other along the way. While it is true that we must walk our path alone on our journey to find ourselves, we also have others to help us along the way. We have our loved ones to keep us company and encourage us on our journey. They just can't walk it for you. YOU have to do the steps, the walking. They have their own steps to walk. And just because a person is on a different path than yours, doesn't mean that they are lost. They have their own self to find there while you are finding yourself there, again and again. A kinder, more loving saying than that of "lead, follow, or get out of the way!" is attributed to Albert Camus, and states, *"Don't walk in front of me, I may not follow. Don't walk behind, I may not lead. Walk beside me and just be my friend."*[35] That's really all we can truly ask of another person on our path to finding ourselves there.

A POEM IN PROGRESS
By Melissa L. Ross

Some days I feel broken,
Other days I'm a bit cracked,
But most days I feel just a little out of whack.
I've never felt normal,
And I've stopped expecting to,
I accept that I think a little differently,
than most other people do.
Maybe being odd isn't all that bad?
So what if it's therapy and a few meds I must add.
I do my best to keep my demons at bay,
And know that there's not always truth
in what my mind has to say.
My self-talk can be brutal,
And for this, I don't know why,
Because I know I'm a good person and I try never to lie.
If I am to trust and believe what people say who love me,
When I look in the mirror, I should try
to see the "me" that they see.
It's true my brain's been damaged,
And my memory's not the same,
But, as long as I have breath in me,
I know I'm still in the game.
Maybe I'm not as crazy, as I often think,
I'll have to double check on that, the
next time I see my shrink.

THE SEMICOLON PROJECT

I would like to mention the importance of the semicolon project, and pay homage to its founder, Amy Bleuel. Project Semicolon[36] is a global non-profit organization that was started in the spring of 2013, by Amy Bleuel, who wanted to honor her father, whom she lost to suicide. Through the semicolon symbol, many related to the struggle of depression, addiction, self-injury, and suicide and their will to continue on; to believe that this is not the end, but a new beginning.

The semicolon represents a sentence where the author could have ended their story, but chose not to. "The author is you and the sentence is your life. You are choosing to keep going."

Tragically, on March 23, 2017, Amy Bleuel, age 31, passed away, having lost her battle with depression to suicide. But, her message of hope and encouragement lives on in the countless lives of others still struggling who have found their own strength to continue their stories, by Amy speaking out about her father's depression, and her own. Project Semicolon was started "one day, by one girl, who told her story, and that story changed the world."[37] Please visit Project Semicolon, and help continue to spread awareness. The more awareness and education we spread about mental illness, the less shame sufferers will feel about speaking out. Through telling our own stories, and listening to the stories of fellow sufferers, we can identify with others, and not feel so alone. Through this brave act of sharing, we can also encourage each other to get the help we need to courageously continue our journeys.

"My Story Isn't Over Yet;"

AND NEITHER IS YOURS;

**THIS BOOK IS DEDICATED TO
THE LOVING MEMORY
OF OUR FURRY BOY CAT, ZOEY.**

September 1, 2001- April 1, 2017

"You are so sadly gone from our lives but
will forever be remembered, deeply loved and
severely missed in our minds and hearts."

Our boy, Zoey

ENDNOTES

1   Ram Dass, *Ram Dass – Quotes*, https://www.ramdass.org/ram-dass-quotes/ (Apr. 2, 2015).

2   The Book Resort, *Don't Look Back, You're Not Going That Way - Mary Engelbreit*, http://thebookresort.blogspot.com/2009/04/dont-look-back-youre-not-going-that-way.html (Apr. 15, 1999).

3   IMDb, *Alyssa Milano: Quotes*, http://m.imdb.com/name/nm0000192/quotes (accessed May 14, 2017).

4   Jon Kabat-Zinn, *Wherever You Go, There You Are* (New York: Hyperion, 2005).

5   Anxiety and Depression Association of America, *Symptoms of PTSD*, https://www.adaa.org/understanding-anxiety/posttraumatic-stress-disorder-ptsd/symptoms (Apr. 2016).

6   Good Reads, *Akshay Dubey Quotes*, http://www.goodreads.com/quotes/1274987-healing-doesn-t-mean-the-damage-never-existed-it-means-the (accessed May 14, 2017).

7   Mrk 12:31

8   Yes Magazine, *The Ancient Greeks' 6 Words for Love (And Why Knowing Them Can Change Your Life)*, http://www.yesmagazine.org/happiness/the-ancient-greeks-6-words-for-love-and-why-knowing-them-can-change-your-life (Dec. 27, 2013).

9   Believers VS Non-Believers, *Scientist vs. Religious person*, https://believervsnonbelievers.wordpress.com/2015/02/20/scientist-vs-religious-person/ (Feb. 20, 2015).

10 BrainyQuote.com, *Niccolo Machiavelli Quotes*, https://www.brainyquote.com/quotes/quotes/n/niccolomac103757.html (accessed May 14, 2017).

11 Prov 13:24

12 Lev 18:22

13 Matt 5:38-48

14 *Silence of the Lambs*. Dir. Jonathan Demme. Orion Pictures, 1991. Film.

15 Matt 7:7

16 *The Most Hated Woman in America*. Dir. Tommy O'Haver. Brownstone Productions, 2017. Film.

17 BrainyQuote.com, *James Thurber Quotes*, https://www. brainyquote.com/quotes/quotes/j/jamesthurb106488.html (accessed May 14, 2017).

18 Good Reads, *Dalai Lama XIV Quotes*, http://www.goodreads. com/quotes/253991-people-take-different-roads-seeking-fulfillment-and-happiness-just-because (accessed May 14, 2017).

19 Boundless, *Freudian Psychoanalytic Theory of Personality*. https://www.boundless.com/psychology/textbooks/boundless-psychology-textbook/personality-16/psychodynamic-perspectives-on-personality-77/freudian-psychoanalytic-theory-of-personality-304-12839/ (accessed May 6, 2017).

20 https://www.boundless.com/psychology/textbooks/ boundless-psychology-textbook/personality-16/ psychodynamic-perspectives-on-personality-77/ freudian-psychoanalytic-theory-of-personality-304-12839/

21 https://www.boundless.com/psychology/textbooks/ boundless-psychology-textbook/personality-16/ psychodynamic-perspectives-on-personality-77/ freudian-psychoanalytic-theory-of-personality-304-12839/

22 AllPsych.com, *Psychology 101, Chapter 3: Section 5: Freud's Structural and Topographical Model*, https://allpsych.com/ psychology101/ego/ (Apr. 1, 2001).

23 Good Reads, *Bryan White Quotes*, http://www.goodreads. com/quotes/21520-people-never-grow-up-they-just-learn-how-to-act (accessed May 14, 2017).

24 Eric Berne, *Games People Play* (New York: Ballantine Books, 1996).

25 https://www.boundless.com/psychology/textbooks/ boundless-psychology-textbook/personality-16/

psychodynamic-perspectives-on-personality-77/
freudian-psychoanalytic-theory-of-personality-304-12839/

26 Wikipedia, *Maslow's hierarchy of needs*, https://en.wikipedia.
org/wiki/Maslow%27s_hierarchy_of_needs (accessed May 14,
2017).

27 *Carrie*. Dir. Brian De Palma. Red Bank Films, 1976. Film.

28 The Brighthill Lantern, *The Inner Child*, http://brighthill.net/
the-inner-child (accessed May 14, 2017).

29 http://brighthill.net/the-inner-child

30 Boundless, *Erikson's Stages of Psychosocial Development*,
https://www.boundless.com/psychology/textbooks/boundless-
psychology-textbook/human-development-14/theories-of-
human-development-70/erikson-s-stages-of-psychosocial-
development-269-12804/ (Sep. 20, 2016, accessed May 14,
2017).

31 Good Reads, *Tim Robbins Quotes*, http://www.goodreads.
com/quotes/53327-it-s-never-too-late-to-have-a-happy-
childhood (Accessed May 14, 2017).

32 J. R. R. Tolkien, *The Hobbit* (Boston: Houghton Mifflin
Harcourt, 2012)

33 Wikipedia, *George Santayana*, https://en.wikiquote.org/wiki/
George_Santayana (accessed May 14, 2017).

34 BrainyQuote.com, *Robert Byrne Quotes*, https://www.
brainyquote.com/quotes/quotes/r/robertbyrn101054.html
(accessed May 14, 2017).

35 BrainyQuote.com, *Albert Camus Quotes*, https://www.
brainyquote.com/quotes/quotes/a/albertcamu100779.html
(accessed May 14, 2017).

36 Project Semicolon, https://projectsemicolon.com/ (accessed
May 14, 2017).

37 https://projectsemicolon.com/